SEO
STRATEGIES IN THE AGE OF AI

First Edition
SEO Strategies in the Age of AI
Copyright © 2024 by Consultingly, LLC

Author, Cover, Typography
Adam J. Lambert-Gorwyn

Imprint
Independently Published

ISBN: 979-8-34617-787-6

Author's Note

This book is intended for informational purposes only. Names, examples, and case studies are used for illustrative purposes and do not represent endorsements or real-world outcomes. All rights reserved. No part of this book may be reproduced or transmitted in any form without the author's prior permission, except for brief quotations in reviews or permitted uses by copyright law.

> "We're moving from a world where search was about 'finding' to a world where search is about 'understanding.'"
>
> Sundar Pichai
> CEO of Google

Chapter 1. Introduction – The Intersection of SEO and AI

Search engine optimization (SEO) and artificial intelligence (AI) are no longer separate realms; they are converging to shape how users find and interact with information online. This intersection of SEO and AI is transforming how businesses approach visibility, relevance, and user engagement. Traditional SEO focused primarily on keywords and links, but as AI becomes more integral to search engines, factors like user intent, content quality, and personalization are increasingly important. This chapter explores how search engines have evolved from basic algorithms to complex, AI-driven systems and examines the impact of AI on search behavior and expectations. As we set the foundation for this guide, you'll gain insight into why AI-driven SEO matters and what it means for optimizing digital presence.

A. The Evolution of Search Engines

To understand how SEO is changing, we need to look back at where it began. In the early days, search engines were relatively straightforward. They relied on simple algorithms designed to identify keywords on web pages and rank them based on how frequently those terms appeared. The thinking was: if a page had the keywords you were searching for, it was probably relevant to your query. In those days, SEO largely meant repeating keywords and building as many links as possible—strategies that seem crude by today's standards.

As search evolved, so did the tactics that worked. Google entered the scene with a groundbreaking approach:

PageRank, an algorithm that considered not just keywords but the number and quality of links pointing to a page. This new algorithm was designed to rank content by its authority and relevance, prioritizing pages that were cited by other reputable sites. Suddenly, SEO wasn't just about packing in keywords; it was about establishing credibility.

With each advancement, search engines have increasingly emphasized *context* over *content quantity*. They're designed to think beyond the surface and look at the broader themes of content, not just isolated terms.

From Keywords to Contextual Understanding

By the mid-2000s, search engines started looking beyond keywords and developed the ability to understand *context*—an approach that would lay the groundwork for modern SEO. With advances in machine learning, search engines began to comprehend topics and phrases in relation to one another. This led to the idea of *semantic search*, which focuses on the *meaning* behind the words, not just the words themselves.

Consider a search for "best running shoes." A simple algorithm would prioritize pages that repeated "best running shoes" the most. A semantic, context-aware search engine, on the other hand, recognizes that related terms like "top-rated athletic footwear" or "shoes for long-distance running" are also relevant.

The Rise of AI-Powered Systems: The Next Evolution of Search

AI has transformed search engines from being responsive tools to proactive assistants. AI systems don't just react to searches—they learn, adapt, and anticipate. For example, algorithms like Google's RankBrain and BERT leverage AI to interpret more complex queries, even those in conversational or question-based formats. This marks a huge shift, as these AI-driven systems are better at understanding nuance, synonyms, and context within phrases.

Today, AI-driven search engines strive to deliver the *best answer* rather than just a matching page. By learning from user behavior—how people phrase questions, the results they click on, and the content they spend time reading—AI algorithms continuously refine their understanding of human intent. This means that optimizing for AI-driven search goes beyond inserting the right keywords; it requires understanding the user's needs and providing answers that feel relevant, clear, and valuable.

SEO in the AI Era: What It Means for You

As search engines evolve, so must our approach to SEO. It's no longer just a technical discipline; it's about truly connecting with people. You're optimizing for machines that understand human language and behavior on a deep level. That means your content needs to be as helpful as possible while staying authentic to your brand.

Today, SEO isn't just about visibility—it's about *resonance*. As AI continues to shape the way people search, optimizing for AI-powered systems will involve meeting users' needs in a way that's intuitive, empathetic, and relevant. The chapters ahead will explore strategies and techniques to help you navigate this exciting intersection of SEO and AI, equipping you to build a future-proof approach that aligns with both search engines and the people who use them.

B. The Impact of AI on Search Behavior

Changes in User Interaction and Expectations

As AI reshapes search, it's also transforming how people interact with search engines and what they expect from them. The days of typing short, basic keywords are long gone. Today, people are increasingly speaking to their devices as if they're asking a human question, trusting that they'll receive a relevant, helpful answer. This shift is a direct response to AI's capabilities—and it's setting a new standard for how search engines need to perform.

1. The Shift to Conversational Queries

One of the most visible changes AI has brought to search is the rise of conversational queries. With the popularity of voice-activated assistants like Siri, Google Assistant, and Alexa, users are increasingly speaking full sentences or even complex questions into their devices. Instead of typing "weather Tokyo," they'll ask, "What's the weather like in Tokyo this weekend?" This shift means that search engines must interpret the *intent* behind natural language, understanding context, phrasing, and even tone to return accurate answers.

This change requires a more sophisticated approach to SEO. Optimizing for conversational queries isn't about choosing the right keywords; it's about creating content that mirrors how people speak, using question-based headings and conversational language. For businesses, this means rethinking how content is structured—focusing on the questions your audience is likely to ask and ensuring your content provides direct, easy-to-understand answers.

2. Users Expect Immediate, Accurate, and Actionable Answers

Users expect fast, precise answers. Whether they're searching for product recommendations, local businesses, or how-to guides, people want solutions without having to sift through multiple sources. Search engines now strive to deliver "zero-click" answers—those quick summaries or featured snippets that provide users with immediate information at the top of the results page.

For businesses, this means that SEO success isn't just about ranking highly; it's about positioning content to become the *primary answer* that AI-driven search engines display. Featured snippets, for example, are a coveted spot that AI-driven algorithms often prioritize. To claim this space, it's essential to create concise, structured answers that address users' needs directly and effectively.

3. Personalization: AI's Role in Tailoring Results to Individual Users

AI has made personalization a core component of modern search. Based on users' past behavior, search engines can now tailor results to align more closely with individual preferences, location, search history, and even browsing habits. For example, someone who frequently searches for healthy recipes might see different results for "quick dinner ideas" than someone who typically searches for comfort food. AI algorithms recognize these patterns and serve results that they anticipate will match each user's tastes and lifestyle.

This personalization influences SEO strategy on several levels. Content must be relevant not just broadly, but to specific user segments. Additionally, this trend emphasizes the importance of a consistent, recognizable brand voice and identity that resonates with target audiences across all touchpoints, as AI will likely favor brands with a strong track record of user engagement.

4. Greater Emphasis on User Experience (UX)

Finally, AI-driven search has significantly raised the bar for user experience. Fast loading times, mobile-friendly designs, and intuitive site navigation aren't just nice-to-have features; they're critical factors that affect rankings. Google's Core Web Vitals, for example, measure aspects of user experience—such as loading speed, interactivity, and visual stability—that directly impact search rankings.

For businesses, this means investing in a seamless user experience across all devices, which ultimately influences how AI-driven search engines assess and rank your site. Ensuring that your site is fast, accessible, and user-friendly isn't just a technical SEO requirement; it's a fundamental way to meet the expectations of today's search users, who have come to expect a smooth, efficient browsing experience.

C. Purpose and Scope of This Guide

What Readers Will Learn and Achieve

SEO is no longer just a matter of optimizing for keywords or backlinks. With AI-driven technologies fundamentally changing how search engines operate and users interact, traditional approaches to SEO need to adapt to remain effective. This guide is designed to bridge that gap, offering a comprehensive roadmap to understanding and thriving in the era of AI-enhanced search.

Whether you're a business owner, digital marketer, or SEO professional, this book will equip you with the insights and strategies you need to navigate the AI-driven future of search. Here's what you can expect to learn and achieve:

1. Understand the Fundamentals of AI-Driven Search

We'll start by exploring the core principles of how search engines work and why AI is a game-changer. You'll gain an understanding of the evolution of search technology, including the shift from basic algorithms to sophisticated AI systems that interpret context, intent, and user behavior. By grasping these foundational concepts, you'll be able to better understand the "why" behind AI's impact on SEO and the strategies you'll implement.

2. Master Over 200 Key SEO Ranking Factors

SEO is made up of hundreds of factors, from on-page elements and technical optimizations to user experience and backlink quality. This guide breaks down these factors into clear, actionable categories, allowing you to understand which ones have the greatest impact in an AI-driven environment. You'll learn which ranking factors to prioritize and how each affects your visibility across both traditional and AI-enhanced search platforms.

3. Develop AI-Optimized Content Strategies

Content is at the heart of any SEO strategy, but AI has redefined what "optimized content" looks like. We'll delve into AI-friendly content creation techniques, from using structured data and entity optimization to writing for conversational, question-based searches. You'll discover how to create content that not only ranks well but resonates with the way users search and interact with AI-powered platforms today.

4. Optimize for Conversational and Voice Search

Voice search has rapidly changed how people phrase their queries and what they expect from search results. In this guide, you'll learn how to adapt your SEO strategy to meet the unique demands of voice search and natural language queries. By incorporating techniques for capturing voice-driven queries, you'll be better prepared to capture this growing segment of search traffic.

5. Build a Holistic SEO Strategy for AI and Traditional Search

One of the unique challenges of the AI era is balancing optimization for both AI-driven and traditional search engines. This guide provides a holistic approach to SEO, enabling you to blend technical optimizations with engaging, human-centered content. You'll learn how to create an SEO strategy that addresses the needs of AI algorithms without losing the personal touch that keeps users engaged.

6. Leverage Advanced SEO Tools and AI-Powered Insights

AI itself offers powerful tools that can enhance your SEO efforts, from keyword research to predictive analytics. This guide covers the best AI-powered tools available today, helping you automate, optimize, and measure your SEO strategies. You'll gain practical insights into how these tools work and how to use them effectively to save time, enhance accuracy, and improve your search performance.

7. Measure Success and Continuously Improve Your Strategy

Finally, successful SEO is a process of continuous improvement. You'll learn how to set measurable goals, track your progress, and refine your approach based on data-driven insights. This guide will provide you with frameworks for assessing the impact of your strategies, ensuring that you can adapt and evolve as AI technology and search behaviors continue to advance.

By the end of this book, you'll be equipped with the tools, knowledge, and strategies needed to navigate the complexities of SEO in an AI-driven world. You'll understand the forces shaping modern search, know how to adapt your website and content to meet evolving standards, and feel confident in your ability to stay ahead.

This guide is your complete resource for mastering SEO in the age of AI—whether you're just starting out or looking to enhance your existing strategy.

Chapter 2. Demystifying Search Engine Logic

Search engines have evolved far beyond their early days of simple keyword matching. Today, they operate using highly complex algorithms designed to understand, interpret, and rank content based on relevance, authority, and user experience. For businesses and content creators, knowing how search engines analyze, categorize, and prioritize information is crucial for crafting effective SEO strategies. In this chapter, we will demystify the inner workings of search engines, exploring the foundational processes of crawling, indexing, and ranking, along with the underlying philosophy that drives search algorithms. By understanding these processes, you'll gain the knowledge needed to align your content with the expectations of both users and search engines, setting the stage for improved visibility and engagement.

A. How Search Engines Work

Crawling, Indexing, and Ranking Processes

To understand how to optimize for search engines, it's essential to know how they operate under the hood. Search engines like Google, Bing, and others follow a three-stage process—crawling, indexing, and ranking—to organize, interpret, and display the vast amount of information available online. Each step plays a crucial role in determining how content is discovered and ranked, and understanding these steps can help you align your SEO efforts with the way search engines think.

1. Crawling: Discovering New and Updated Content

The first stage of the search engine process is *crawling*. In this phase, search engines send out *crawlers* or *bots* (often called "spiders") to explore and discover new or updated content across the web. These bots move from link to link, scanning pages and collecting information. They essentially "crawl" the internet continuously, aiming to locate every piece of content they can access.

- **How Crawling Works**: Crawlers start with a list of known URLs, often including sitemaps that websites submit directly to search engines. From there, they follow internal and external links, discovering new pages and updated content. This process is ongoing, meaning that crawlers are constantly updating their understanding of what content is available online.

- **Why Crawling Matters for SEO**: If your content isn't crawlable, it might as well be invisible to search engines. Ensuring that your site structure is clear, links are functional, and navigation is intuitive helps crawlers find and understand your pages. For SEO, submitting a sitemap and using a logical link structure are essential practices that make it easier for crawlers to do their job efficiently.

2. Indexing: Organizing and Storing Information

Once a page is crawled, the next step is *indexing*. This is where search engines process and organize the information gathered from crawling. The content of each page is analyzed to determine what it's about, then it's stored in a massive database called the *index*. This index serves as the foundation for search results, allowing search engines to retrieve relevant pages quickly when a user enters a query.

- **How Indexing Works**: During indexing, search engines extract important elements from a page—such as text, images, and metadata—and categorize them by keywords and topics. They analyze signals like the frequency of keywords, the page's structure, and its context to understand the content. Content that aligns with recognized topics or entities may also be linked to those broader concepts within the index.

- **Why Indexing Matters for SEO**: Only indexed content can appear in search results. If your content isn't indexed, it won't show up in searches, no matter how relevant it might be. To ensure that your content gets indexed, use clear and relevant titles, metadata, and headings that help search engines categorize it effectively. It's also crucial to avoid duplicate content, as this can confuse search engines and potentially lead to lower rankings.

3. Ranking: Deciding What to Display and in What Order

The final stage is *ranking*, where the search engine decides the order in which to display results for a given query. This is where the hundreds of ranking factors come into play. Search engines use complex algorithms to evaluate the relevance, authority, and quality of each indexed page and assign a ranking to it based on those criteria. The goal is to present the most relevant, helpful, and trustworthy information first.

- **How Ranking Works**: When a user submits a query, the search engine scans its index to find pages that match. It then evaluates those pages based on various ranking factors—such as keyword relevance, backlinks, site structure, and user experience—to determine their position on the results page. AI and machine learning algorithms, like Google's RankBrain and BERT, also play a role in interpreting the intent behind queries, especially for conversational or complex questions.

- **Why Ranking Matters for SEO**: Ranking determines where your content appears in search results, which directly affects visibility and traffic. To improve your chances of ranking highly, focus on optimizing for key ranking factors like quality content, user experience, and authority. Additionally, understand that ranking algorithms are continuously updated, which means staying current with SEO best practices is essential for maintaining your site's performance.

Understanding How Search Engines Work: Key Takeaways

By grasping the basics of crawling, indexing, and ranking, you can take a proactive approach to ensure that your content is visible, accessible, and competitive. Think of each stage as a checkpoint in your SEO strategy. First, make sure your content can be crawled, so it's discoverable. Then, optimize your content for indexing by using clear titles and relevant metadata. Finally, target ranking by creating high-quality, relevant content that aligns with user intent.

With a strong understanding of these processes, you're setting up a solid foundation for SEO success. In the following chapters, we'll dive into the specific strategies, tools, and techniques that can help you optimize for each stage, ensuring your content performs well across the full search engine lifecycle.

B. The Philosophy Behind Search Algorithms

Relevance, Authority, and User Satisfaction

Search engines are designed with a fundamental goal: to connect users with the information they need as quickly and accurately as possible. To achieve this, algorithms assess millions of web pages to determine which ones best meet a user's query. At the heart of this process lie three core principles: *relevance*, *authority*, and *user satisfaction*. These principles guide how search engines evaluate and rank content, creating the foundation for SEO strategies that focus on quality and user-centered design.

1. Relevance: Matching Content to User Intent

Relevance is the first and most essential consideration for search engines. When a user enters a query, the algorithm's primary task is to determine which pages offer content that matches the intent behind that query. Search engines have evolved to look beyond simple keyword matches, seeking to understand context and meaning to identify pages that best align with what the user is actually looking for.

- **How Relevance is Determined**: Search engines assess relevance by analyzing keywords and their context within a page, identifying related terms, and understanding the overall topic. Algorithms like Google's BERT and RankBrain use natural language processing to interpret complex or conversational queries, ensuring that results accurately match the intent behind the words.

- **Why Relevance Matters for SEO**: Optimizing for relevance means creating content that aligns closely with the questions and needs of your target audience.

This requires a deep understanding of user intent and the types of queries your content is likely to satisfy. Focusing on creating content that directly addresses specific, real-world questions will improve your site's relevance, increasing the chances that it will be prioritized by search algorithms.

2. Authority: Establishing Trust and Credibility

Authority refers to a site's perceived credibility and expertise within its field. Search engines aim to prioritize content from sources that demonstrate knowledge, reliability, and trustworthiness. In assessing authority, search engines look at signals such as the quality of inbound links (backlinks) and the site's historical performance. Content from established, reputable sources is generally ranked higher because it's more likely to provide accurate, trustworthy information.

- **How Authority is Determined**: Authority is often measured by analyzing a site's backlink profile. High-quality backlinks from reputable sites signal that others find your content valuable, which can elevate your site's authority. Other factors, such as brand mentions, social signals, and domain history, also contribute to how a site's authority is perceived by search engines.

- **Why Authority Matters for SEO**: Building authority involves developing content that's not only valuable to your audience but recognized by other credible sources. Earning backlinks from trusted sites, providing expert insights, and establishing a consistent brand voice all contribute to strengthening your authority. Over time, this positions your site as a credible source within your industry, which boosts your chances of ranking higher for competitive keywords.

3. User Satisfaction: Prioritizing Positive User Experiences

User satisfaction has become a vital factor in modern search algorithms. Search engines aim to promote pages that not only provide relevant and authoritative content but also deliver a positive user experience. Factors like page load speed, mobile responsiveness, and user engagement metrics (such as time on page and bounce rate) help search engines gauge how satisfying a page is for visitors.

- **How User Satisfaction is Measured**: Search engines use various metrics to evaluate user satisfaction. Core Web Vitals, for instance, measure aspects of page load speed, interactivity, and visual stability. Engagement signals, such as low bounce rates, long session durations, and high click-through rates, indicate that users find the content useful and enjoyable to interact with.

- **Why User Satisfaction Matters for SEO**: Optimizing for user satisfaction involves creating a seamless, enjoyable experience for visitors. This means not only providing valuable content but also ensuring that your site is easy to navigate, visually appealing, and accessible on all devices. A positive user experience increases engagement and builds trust, signaling to search engines that your site is worthy of higher rankings.

Bringing It All Together: The Balance of Relevance, Authority, and User Satisfaction

These three principles—relevance, authority, and user satisfaction—are interdependent, each reinforcing the others to create a balanced and effective SEO strategy. While relevance ensures that your content aligns with user needs, authority builds the credibility needed for search engines to trust your site, and user satisfaction confirms that your content delivers on its promise.

In practice, successful SEO means optimizing for all three elements. Focus on creating meaningful, high-quality content that directly addresses your audience's needs, work to build authority within your industry, and invest in user experience improvements to keep visitors engaged. By aligning with these core principles, you're not only improving your search rankings but also building a sustainable, user-centered approach to SEO that adapts well to ongoing algorithm updates and continual change.

C. The Role of AI in Modern Search Engines

Machine Learning, NLP, and Personalization

Artificial Intelligence (AI) has revolutionized search engines, transforming them from basic tools that matched keywords to complex systems that understand, anticipate, and respond to human needs. AI technologies like Machine Learning (ML), Natural Language Processing (NLP), and personalization are integral to how modern search engines operate. These advancements enable search engines to deliver results that are more accurate, context-aware, and tailored to each user, changing the way SEO professionals approach optimization.

1. Machine Learning: The Engine of Constant Improvement

Machine Learning is a core AI technology that allows search engines to learn and adapt based on vast amounts of data. Unlike traditional algorithms, which rely on static rules, ML algorithms analyze patterns in user behavior, search queries, and content to refine results continually. The more data the search engine processes, the better it becomes at identifying relevant results and predicting what users are looking for.

- **How Machine Learning Works in Search**: Search engines use ML to process billions of daily interactions, identifying patterns in user queries, click behavior, and content quality. Google's RankBrain, one of the first widely recognized ML applications in search, helps the algorithm interpret unfamiliar or complex queries by identifying similar patterns from past searches. Over time, ML systems "learn" which results are most relevant for different types of queries, allowing them to handle even ambiguous or novel searches effectively.

- **Why Machine Learning Matters for SEO**: Because ML algorithms are constantly evolving, SEO is no longer a set-and-forget process. Businesses must adopt an agile approach, regularly monitoring performance and refining their strategies. SEO professionals can leverage insights from search trends and user behavior to inform content and optimization strategies, aligning them with the algorithm's learning curve. Staying adaptable is key, as ML-driven updates can impact rankings unexpectedly but often reward high-quality, user-centered content.

2. Natural Language Processing (NLP): Understanding Context and Meaning

Natural Language Processing allows search engines to interpret language more naturally, which is crucial as queries become longer and more conversational. With NLP, search engines don't just match words—they understand *context*, *intent*, and *relationships* between terms. This ability to process natural language has transformed how search engines respond to questions, particularly complex or conversational queries.

- **How NLP Works in Search**: NLP analyzes the structure and semantics of language, enabling the algorithm to understand phrases and sentences as a human would. Google's BERT (Bidirectional Encoder Representations from Transformers) algorithm is a landmark in NLP for search. BERT helps Google understand context by analyzing the relationships between words, even considering prepositions like "for" or "to" to interpret the intent behind a query accurately. For example, in the search "best books for learning Spanish," BERT understands that the user wants resources for language learning, not books written in Spanish.

- **Why NLP Matters for SEO**: With NLP, SEO is about more than just targeting keywords; it's about understanding user intent. To optimize for NLP-driven algorithms, content should be structured to answer questions and provide comprehensive, topic-focused information. Using a conversational tone and incorporating long-tail keywords or question-based headings can help align content with the ways users phrase queries. This approach allows content to rank for a broader range of relevant queries, meeting users where they are in their search journey.

3. Personalization: Tailoring Results to Individual Users

AI-powered personalization has made search experiences uniquely tailored to each user, factoring in elements like location, search history, device, and even the time of day. By analyzing this data, search engines can deliver results that are more relevant to each individual, enhancing user satisfaction and engagement.

- **How Personalization Works in Search**: Personalization algorithms use AI to filter results based on what they know about the user. For example, if a user frequently searches for vegan recipes, the algorithm will prioritize vegan content in future food-related queries. Similarly, local search results are influenced by the user's location, surfacing nearby businesses for relevant queries. Personalization also adjusts for device type, prioritizing mobile-optimized sites for users searching on mobile devices.

- **Why Personalization Matters for SEO**: For SEO, personalization means focusing on user-specific factors that can influence visibility. Creating localized content, optimizing for mobile, and understanding user segments all contribute to improving rankings for personalized results. By crafting content that caters to distinct user groups or regional audiences, businesses can better capture traffic from personalized searches. Additionally, being aware of trends in user behavior, such as popular queries or seasonal interests, helps create content that resonates more deeply with targeted audiences.

AI in Modern Search: A Paradigm Shift for SEO

Machine Learning, NLP, and personalization represent a paradigm shift in how search engines interpret, rank, and present content. With these technologies, search engines are not just responding to keywords; they're engaging in a sophisticated process of understanding users as individuals with specific needs and preferences.

For SEO professionals, the role of AI means adopting a more nuanced, responsive approach to optimization. Effective SEO in this environment isn't just about ranking highly; it's about delivering content that genuinely serves the user. This requires aligning with the ways search engines understand language and context, while also recognizing the factors that make each user's search experience unique.

Chapter 3. Important Ranking Factors

Achieving high search rankings involves more than just focusing on a few core SEO principles. Search engines analyze a vast array of factors—over 200 in total—to determine the relevance, quality, and authority of content. These factors range from technical details like site speed and mobile-friendliness to content depth, user engagement metrics, and the strength of a website's backlink profile. This chapter provides a comprehensive breakdown of these ranking factors, categorized into on-page, off-page, technical, user-specific, and content-related elements. By understanding and optimizing for these diverse factors, you'll be better equipped to boost your site's performance in search results, ensuring it meets both search engine standards and user expectations.

A. On-Page SEO Factors

1. Content Quality and Relevance

Content quality and relevance are critical for ranking. AI-powered search engines, now capable of understanding user intent and context, prioritize content that demonstrates depth, originality, and value. A key aspect of this is content length, as longer content often has a better chance of meeting the criteria for relevance and comprehensiveness. Research suggests that articles in the 1,500-2,000 word range tend to perform well because they provide enough information to satisfy user intent and meet the search engine's criteria for quality. Below, we'll explore the essential elements of content quality: originality, depth, value, and length.

Originality: Creating Unique and Insightful Content

Originality is foundational to ranking well. Search engines penalize duplicate content because it doesn't add unique value for users. Original content demonstrates authority and insight, setting a website apart as a trusted source.

- **Why Originality Matters**: Duplicate content dilutes a website's ability to rank well, while original, high-quality content helps establish trust and authority. Unique perspectives and data can boost user engagement and signal to search engines that your content offers something fresh.

- **How to Achieve Originality**: Avoid simply rehashing existing information; instead, offer new insights, original research, or unique takes on common topics. For example, if your content covers "digital marketing best practices," add depth by including real-world case studies or specific industry examples. This ensures your content is valuable and sets you apart from competitors who may cover the same topic in a more generic way.

Depth: Providing Comprehensive, Thorough Information

Content depth is essential in the AI era, as users expect fully developed answers to their questions. In-depth content shows search engines that your page provides authoritative coverage of a topic, a crucial factor in ranking.

- **Why Depth Matters**: Content that lacks depth may lead to higher bounce rates as users leave to find more comprehensive answers elsewhere. Search engines track these engagement signals and favor pages that keep users engaged. A detailed approach can result in higher dwell time, which positively impacts rankings.

- **How to Achieve Depth**: Use topic clusters to cover a subject comprehensively, with clear subheadings that address related questions. For instance, if you're writing about "content marketing strategies," explore subtopics like content creation, distribution, and performance measurement. This layered structure improves user experience and increases your chances of ranking for multiple related keywords, capturing a broader range of searches.

Value: Delivering Information That Meets User Needs

Valuable content is user-centered, designed to address specific goals, challenges, or questions that users have. In an AI-driven search environment, value is often measured by engagement metrics, such as time on page, shares, and clicks.

- **Why Value Matters**: Content that is seen as valuable builds brand loyalty and has a better chance of generating high engagement metrics, such as low bounce rates and higher time on page. AI algorithms prioritize content that consistently engages users, as it signals user satisfaction.

- **How to Deliver Value**: Begin by understanding your audience's needs and goals. Create actionable, insightful content that addresses these needs directly. For instance, if your audience is searching for "how to create an SEO strategy," provide actionable steps, examples, and insights that go beyond basic advice. This approach increases the likelihood that your content will be bookmarked, shared, and revisited.

Content Length: Crafting Long-Form Content That Adds Depth

Studies suggest that content length is an influential factor in SEO. Research from sources like Backlinko and HubSpot indicates that articles in the 1,500-2,000 word range often perform better in search rankings. This is because longer content is more likely to cover a topic thoroughly, increasing relevance, authority, and user satisfaction.

- **Why Content Length Matters**: Longer content allows for greater depth, which helps capture user intent more comprehensively. Content in the 1,500-2,000 word range has been shown to attract more backlinks and encourage longer dwell times. According to a Backlinko study, the average first-page result on Google is approximately 1,447 words long, supporting the correlation between content length and higher rankings.

- **How to Use Content Length Effectively**: Avoid adding words for the sake of it. Ensure each section adds value, covers new angles, or deepens the topic's exploration. For example, if you're writing about "SEO for eCommerce," a longer article could cover keyword research, on-page optimization, link-building strategies, and case studies. This way, content length becomes a natural result of thoroughly addressing all relevant aspects of the topic.

Bringing It All Together: Optimizing Content Quality and Relevance for SEO Success

By focusing on originality, depth, value, and content length, you can create content that aligns with AI-driven search engines' priorities. These elements work together to deliver a user-centered experience, signaling to search engines that your content is not only comprehensive but also valuable and engaging. By providing well-structured, long-form content that answers user questions thoroughly, you enhance your site's relevance and authority—key factors for improving search rankings.

2. Keyword Usage and Optimization

Effective keyword usage remains a fundamental part of on-page SEO, though the strategies have evolved considerably. In the age of AI-driven search engines, keyword optimization involves more than just placing a target word throughout the content. Now, it's about thoughtful placement, balanced density, and the inclusion of related concepts—often called *Latent Semantic Indexing (LSI) keywords*—that help AI understand context. Optimizing keywords correctly enhances your content's relevance and visibility, ensuring it aligns with both search algorithms and user expectations.

Placement: Positioning Keywords Strategically

Where keywords are placed within your content significantly impacts search engine rankings. Strategic placement helps search engines quickly identify the primary focus of your content and understand its relevance.

- **Why Placement Matters**: Placing keywords in high-visibility areas like the title, meta description, headings, and first 100 words of the content signals to search engines that the content's focus aligns with user queries. These areas are weighted more heavily in algorithms, helping search engines categorize the content accurately.

- **How to Optimize Placement**: Include your primary keyword naturally in the title tag, meta description, and H1 heading. The first paragraph of your content should also introduce the main keyword to establish context early. For example, if your content is about "digital marketing trends," place this phrase in your title, meta description, and opening lines. Additionally, using the primary keyword in subheadings (H2, H3) as appropriate reinforces topic relevance without excessive repetition.

Density: Maintaining a Natural Keyword Frequency

Keyword density, or the frequency of keywords in your content, should strike a balance that emphasizes relevance without appearing forced. Excessive keyword usage, known as "keyword stuffing," can harm user experience and may lead to penalties from search engines. Instead, aim for a natural density that supports readability while reinforcing the topic.

- **Why Density Matters**: Search engines penalize overuse of keywords as it can make content appear spammy and diminish user experience. Conversely, not using keywords frequently enough may make it harder for search engines to recognize your content's focus. A balanced density optimizes relevance while ensuring the content flows naturally for readers.

- **How to Maintain Optimal Density**: Aim for a keyword density of around 1-2%—typically once every 100-150 words—as a general rule, but focus on readability. For example, if writing a 1,500-word article, using the main keyword 10-15 times within the content should suffice. However, instead of fixating on precise numbers, ensure keywords appear organically where they naturally fit, such as in examples, and summaries.

LSI Keywords: Incorporating Related Terms and Concepts

Latent Semantic Indexing (LSI) keywords are conceptually related terms and phrases that enrich your content by adding context and depth. LSI keywords help search engines understand the broader topic your content addresses, allowing it to surface your content for a variety of related searches and improve relevance for nuanced queries.

- **Why LSI Keywords Matter**: By using semantically related keywords, you're helping AI-powered algorithms like Google's BERT and RankBrain comprehend the context and relationships within your content. LSI keywords ensure that your content appears for variations of user searches, as search engines recognize these terms as associated with your main topic.

- **How to Find and Use LSI Keywords**: Identify LSI keywords by researching related terms, synonyms, and commonly associated phrases. Tools like LSIGraph, Google's "People Also Ask" suggestions, and AnswerThePublic can help uncover relevant keywords to incorporate. For example, if your main keyword is "content marketing," relevant LSI terms might include "digital marketing strategy," "audience engagement," and "brand storytelling." Integrate these naturally throughout your content, especially in sections where they add clarity or reinforce subtopics.

Bringing It All Together: A Balanced Approach to Keyword Optimization

Effective keyword usage in modern SEO means balancing placement, density, and related terms to ensure content is both user-friendly and aligned with AI-driven algorithms. By positioning keywords strategically, maintaining a natural density, and enriching content with LSI keywords, you make it easier for search engines to understand the focus and context of your content. This approach enhances the likelihood of ranking well for targeted queries and improves overall content relevance for a broader range of searches.

3. HTML Tags and Meta Data

HTML tags and metadata are essential components of on-page SEO, providing search engines with key information about the structure, focus, and hierarchy of your content. Properly optimized HTML tags, including title tags, meta descriptions, and header tags, help search engines interpret the relevance of your content and make it more compelling for users in search results. By strategically using these elements, you can improve your site's visibility, click-through rates (CTR), and overall user experience.

Title Tags: Crafting Clear, Compelling Titles

Title tags are among the most important on-page SEO elements. This tag is what appears as the clickable headline in search results, and it's often the first impression users and search engines get of your content. A well-crafted title tag should be concise, descriptive, and include the primary keyword to signal relevance.

- **Why Title Tags Matter**: Title tags play a significant role in search engine rankings and CTR. Search engines give considerable weight to title tags in determining a page's relevance to a query. Additionally, a clear and enticing title tag can attract more clicks from users, which further signals value to search engines.

- **How to Optimize Title Tags**: Aim to keep title tags under 60 characters to prevent truncation in search results, and place the main keyword near the beginning for maximum impact. Use action words or questions to make the title more engaging, and be specific about what users can expect. For instance, instead of "Marketing Tips for Businesses," a more optimized title tag could be "10 Essential Marketing Tips for Small Businesses in 2024." This format is concise, includes the main keyword, and communicates value to users right away.

Meta Descriptions: Creating Engaging, Informative Summaries

The meta description is the short snippet that appears under the title tag in search results. Although meta descriptions don't directly impact rankings, they play a crucial role in influencing users' decisions to click. An effective meta description provides a brief, enticing summary of the page content, using language that is both informative and action-oriented.

- **Why Meta Descriptions Matter**: Meta descriptions help improve CTR by giving users a reason to click on your link over others. While not a direct ranking factor, a well-written meta description can increase engagement and drive traffic, which may indirectly boost rankings by signaling user interest to search engines.

- **How to Optimize Meta Descriptions**: Keep meta descriptions within 150-160 characters to avoid truncation, and make sure to incorporate the primary keyword naturally. Use clear, compelling language that highlights the main benefit of the page or answers a question. For example, if the title tag is "10 Essential Marketing Tips for Small Businesses," the meta description could read, "Discover top strategies to grow your small business in 2024 with these actionable marketing tips. Increase engagement, drive sales, and reach your audience effectively." This approach reassures users that the content will deliver on their expectations, making them more likely to click.

Header Tags: Structuring Content for Clarity and SEO

Header tags (H1, H2, H3, etc.) create a logical hierarchy within your content, guiding both users and search engines through the page. These tags are essential for organizing content, signaling the primary and subtopics covered, and breaking up text for improved readability.

- **Why Header Tags Matter**: Search engines use header tags to understand the structure and organization of content. Properly structured headers make it easier for algorithms to determine the main themes of a page, which improves its relevance for specific queries. Additionally, well-organized headers enhance user experience by making content easier to scan and read.

- **How to Optimize Header Tags**: Use only one H1 tag per page, representing the main topic and typically include the primary keyword. Subsequent headers (H2, H3, etc.) should organize subtopics in a logical flow, with H2 tags introducing major sections and H3 or H4 tags used for subpoints. For instance, in an article on "Digital Marketing Strategies," an H1 might be "Effective Digital Marketing Strategies for 2024," with H2s for each major strategy (e.g., "Content Marketing," "Social Media," "SEO"), and H3 tags for specific techniques under each strategy. This hierarchy signals content structure to search engines and makes it easier for users to follow.

Bringing It All Together: Maximizing the Impact of HTML Tags and Meta Data

When used effectively, title tags, meta descriptions, and header tags work together to enhance both search engine visibility and user experience. These elements help search engines understand the relevance of your content while giving users clear, compelling reasons to click through and engage. By strategically optimizing each tag, you're aligning your content with SEO best practices and setting up a strong foundation for attracting and retaining site visitors.

4. User Engagement Metrics

User engagement metrics are vital indicators of how well your content meets user expectations. Search engines like Google increasingly prioritize pages that show high engagement, as these pages are often the ones that best satisfy user intent. Metrics such as *bounce rate*, *time on page*, and *click-through rate (CTR)* reflect how users interact with your content, providing insight into its relevance, quality, and appeal. By understanding and optimizing for these engagement metrics, you can improve not only your search rankings but also the overall user experience.

Bounce Rate: Minimizing Early Exits

Bounce rate is the percentage of visitors who leave your site after viewing only one page. A high bounce rate often indicates that visitors didn't find what they were looking for or were dissatisfied with the content. While some pages, such as blog posts or informational articles, naturally have higher bounce rates, a consistently high bounce rate across key pages can signal a problem to search engines.

- **Why Bounce Rate Matters**: A high bounce rate suggests that users are not engaging deeply with your content, which may indicate a lack of relevance or poor user experience. Search engines view high bounce rates as a sign that a page may not be effectively meeting user intent. A lower bounce rate, on the other hand, often indicates that users find the page valuable and are exploring further.

- **How to Optimize for Bounce Rate**: Start by assessing whether the page content aligns with the expectations set by its title, meta description, and keywords. Make sure your content is immediately engaging and addresses the user's needs right away. Techniques like including clear calls to action, using multimedia (such as images or videos), and improving page load speed can all reduce bounce rates. For example, if you notice a high bounce rate on an informational page, consider adding internal links to related articles or including interactive elements that encourage further exploration.

Time on Page: Encouraging Longer Engagement

Time on page, or dwell time, measures how long users spend on a page before navigating away. A longer time on page generally indicates that visitors are engaged with your content and finding it useful. This metric is especially important for AI-driven search engines, which interpret longer dwell times as a sign of high-quality, relevant content.

- **Why Time on Page Matters**: When users spend more time on a page, it signals to search engines that the content is valuable and satisfying user needs. This can positively impact rankings, as search engines seek to promote pages that keep users engaged. On the flip side, a short time on page may indicate shallow or irrelevant content that doesn't hold users' attention.

- **How to Optimize for Time on Page**: To encourage users to stay longer, focus on creating in-depth, well-structured content that covers the topic comprehensively. Breaking up text with subheadings, images, and videos can improve readability, while interactive features like quizzes or calculators can boost engagement. For example, on a page about "home renovation tips," include real-life examples, checklists, or videos that expand on each tip. The more valuable the content is, the longer users are likely to stay, which signals relevance and quality to search engines.

Click-Through Rate (CTR): Attracting More Clicks in Search Results

Click-through rate (CTR) is the percentage of users who click on your link when it appears in search results. CTR reflects how appealing and relevant your title tags and meta descriptions are, as well as how well they match the user's search intent. Higher CTRs suggest that users find your listing compelling, which can help boost rankings by signaling user interest.

- **Why CTR Matters**: A high CTR shows that your page stands out among other results and that users believe it will provide the information they're seeking. Google and other search engines monitor CTR as an indicator of a page's appeal and relevance for specific queries. Pages with high CTRs often see ranking improvements, as search engines recognize that users are actively choosing them.

- **How to Optimize for CTR**: Craft clear, engaging,

and descriptive title tags and meta descriptions that reflect the content accurately. Include action words or questions to make your titles more appealing and to set clear expectations. For example, if you're targeting the query "best productivity apps," a title tag like "Top 10 Productivity Apps for 2024 to Streamline Your Workflow" combined with a meta description like "Discover the best apps for boosting productivity, from project management to time tracking. Find the right tools for your needs in this comprehensive guide." can increase clicks by appealing directly to user intent.

Bringing It All Together: Optimizing for User Engagement Metrics

Bounce rate, time on page, and CTR are key indicators that help search engines assess how well your content performs in meeting user needs. By optimizing each of these metrics, you're not only improving the SEO of individual pages but also creating a more satisfying experience for users. Engaged users are more likely to stay, explore additional content, and return in the future—outcomes that reinforce your site's authority and relevance in the eyes of search engines.

B. Off-Page SEO Factors

1. Backlink Profile

A strong backlink profile is one of the most critical aspects of off-page SEO, as it directly influences how search engines perceive the authority and credibility of your website. Backlinks, or inbound links from other websites, signal to search engines that your content is valuable and worth referencing. However, not all backlinks are created equal; both the *quality* of links and *anchor text diversity* play a significant role in establishing an effective backlink profile.

Quality vs. Quantity: Prioritizing High-Authority Links

While it may seem beneficial to gather as many backlinks as possible, search engines place a much higher emphasis on the *quality* of links rather than their sheer number. A few backlinks from authoritative, reputable sites can be far more impactful than dozens of low-quality or spammy links. High-quality links come from websites with high domain authority, relevant content, and strong trust signals.

- **Why Quality Matters Over Quantity**: Search engines like Google assess the authority of a website based on its backlink profile. Links from reputable, well-established websites act as a vote of confidence in your content, boosting your own authority. Low-quality links, on the other hand, can harm your rankings. In extreme cases, links from spammy or irrelevant sources may even result in penalties, diminishing your site's credibility.

- **How to Build High-Quality Backlinks**: Focus on earning links from authoritative sites within your industry. Guest blogging on reputable sites, securing mentions in industry publications, and collaborating with influencers are effective strategies. For instance, if your site is about fitness, a backlink from a respected health publication or a popular fitness blog carries significant weight. Tools like Ahrefs or Moz can help identify high-authority sites and track the quality of your backlinks, allowing you to continually refine your link-building strategy.

Anchor Text Diversity: Varying Link Text for Natural Linking Patterns

Anchor text is the clickable text within a link, and it plays an important role in helping search engines understand the context of the link. However, having too many links with identical anchor text can look unnatural to search engines and may raise red flags. A well-rounded backlink profile includes diverse anchor texts that naturally vary to reflect different contexts and content.

- **Why Anchor Text Diversity Matters**: A natural backlink profile typically includes a mix of branded, generic, exact-match, and partial-match anchor texts. Search engines are more likely to view such diversity as a sign of organic linking. Overusing exact-match anchor text (where the anchor text exactly matches the targeted keyword) can appear manipulative and may result in a penalty from search engines.

- **How to Ensure Anchor Text Diversity**: Aim to use a variety of anchor texts in your link-building efforts. For example:
    - **Branded Anchor Text**: Uses your brand name (e.g., "Example Fitness").
    - **Generic Anchor Text**: Uses neutral phrases (e.g., "click here," "learn more").
    - **Exact-Match Anchor Text**: Uses the exact target keyword (e.g., "best workout routines").
    - **Partial-Match Anchor Text**: Uses variations or related phrases (e.g., "top workout tips").

- A balanced approach helps create a natural backlink profile. For instance, if your target keyword is "digital marketing strategies," avoid using this phrase as anchor text for every link. Instead, incorporate variations like "effective marketing tactics" or branded phrases, which will appear more organic.

Bringing It All Together: Building a Balanced Backlink Profile

For off-page SEO, quality backlinks from authoritative sources and diverse anchor text are essential to a strong backlink profile. By prioritizing high-quality links and ensuring a varied, natural anchor text pattern, you signal to search engines that your website is a trusted, credible resource. This, in turn, can improve your rankings and boost organic visibility.

2. Social Signals

Social signals—such as shares, likes, and comments—are increasingly influential in off-page SEO. Although social media activity isn't a direct ranking factor, it does play a critical role in building visibility, credibility, and engagement, which indirectly impacts search engine rankings. A strong social presence can amplify your content, foster user engagement, and drive more traffic to your site, signaling to search engines that your content is valuable and relevant.

Shares: Expanding Reach and Increasing Visibility

Shares are one of the most impactful social signals because they extend your content's reach beyond your immediate audience. When users share your content, it has the potential to go viral, significantly increasing exposure and driving traffic from diverse sources.

- **Why Shares Matter**: Shares indicate that users find your content valuable and worthy of distribution, helping it reach new audiences. This organic sharing contributes to greater visibility and can lead to more backlinks from external sites. High sharing activity can also boost brand authority, as more users interact with and trust your content.

- **How to Encourage Shares**: Make it easy for users to share your content by adding social sharing buttons to your website. Create shareable content—such as informative infographics, engaging videos, or well-researched articles—that provides value to your audience. For instance, a post titled "10 Simple Health Tips for Busy Professionals" is more likely to be shared if it addresses a common need in a concise, visually engaging way. Using clear calls-to-action (CTAs) like "Share with your network" or "Tag a friend who needs this!" can also prompt users to share.

Likes: Validating Content Quality and Appeal

Likes are a quick way for users to show approval, signaling that the content resonates with them. While not as influential as shares, likes still play an important role in social engagement by indicating that your content is interesting and relevant to your audience.

- **Why Likes Matter**: Likes serve as a signal of quality, demonstrating that users find the content appealing. High numbers of likes can boost credibility, encouraging more people to engage with and trust your brand. In social media algorithms, likes often influence the visibility of posts, allowing more people to discover your content and potentially increasing traffic to your website.

- **How to Encourage Likes**: Post content that is visually appealing, informative, and engaging to encourage users to interact. A well-crafted headline, high-quality visuals, or a powerful message can increase the likelihood of receiving likes. For example, eye-catching visuals or quotes from well-known industry figures can encourage users to pause and react to your content. Simple prompts like "Double-tap if you agree" or "Hit the like button if this resonates with you" can also encourage engagement.

Comments: Building Community and Driving Deeper Engagement

Comments represent a deeper level of engagement, as they require users to interact directly with your content. Comments allow users to express their thoughts, ask questions, or start discussions, creating a sense of community and encouraging further interaction.

- **Why Comments Matter**: Comments signal a high level of engagement and interest, indicating that your content sparks conversation and resonates with your audience. A high volume of comments shows search engines and social platforms that your content fosters active engagement, which can improve its visibility on social platforms. Additionally, comments give you valuable insight into your audience's preferences and pain points, allowing you to tailor better content.

- **How to Encourage Comments**: Ask open-ended questions or include prompts that invite feedback to encourage users to comment. For example, ending a post with "What are your thoughts on this?" or "Have you tried this before? Let us know in the comments!" invites users to participate. Engaging with commenters by replying and showing appreciation for their input can further encourage conversation and build a loyal community around your brand.

Bringing It All Together: Leveraging Social Signals for Off-Page SEO Success

Shares, likes, and comments each contribute to a strong social signal profile, boosting visibility and credibility for your content. While social signals don't directly impact SEO rankings, they drive user engagement and website traffic, which indirectly benefit your site's performance. Building a strong social media presence helps your content reach a broader audience, encourages interactions, and positions your brand as an authority.

3. Brand Mentions

Brand mentions—references to your brand name on other websites, whether linked or unlinked—are powerful off-page SEO signals. Unlinked mentions and citations signal credibility and awareness to search engines, even without a direct link. As search engines become more sophisticated in their ability to evaluate online authority and relevance, brand mentions have emerged as an indirect ranking factor that can support your site's visibility and strengthen its online reputation.

Unlinked Mentions: Building Brand Authority Without Backlinks

An *unlinked mention* is when a website or social media platform mentions your brand name without linking directly to your website. These mentions, while lacking a backlink, still contribute to your site's authority by associating your brand with the content or topic in which it's mentioned. Unlinked mentions are becoming more significant as search engines increasingly recognize them as endorsements, especially when they come from reputable sources.

- **Why Unlinked Mentions Matter**: Unlinked mentions provide search engines with additional signals of brand authority and relevance, particularly when they come from high-quality sources. Google's algorithms are now able to interpret brand mentions as indicators of influence, even if there's no direct link. Consistent mentions from trusted sites reinforce your brand's presence and relevance within your industry.

- **How to Generate Unlinked Mentions**: Focus on building relationships with industry publications, influencers, and content creators who are likely to mention your brand. Contribute to guest articles, collaborate on projects, or be quoted as an expert in your field. For example, if your business is a skincare brand, you could collaborate with dermatologists or beauty bloggers who might mention your brand in discussions about skincare tips. Additionally, being active on platforms like Reddit, Quora, and forums can organically create unlinked mentions as users share their experiences with your brand.

Citations: Establishing Trust and Accuracy

Citations refer to references that include your business name, address, phone number, or other key information, often associated with local SEO. Citations are typically found on business directories, review sites, and local listings and are essential for reinforcing your brand's credibility and accuracy. Even without links, citations validate your business's legitimacy, making it easier for search engines to recognize and trust your brand.

- **Why Citations Matter**: Citations help search engines verify your business's authenticity, especially for local searches. Consistent and accurate citations across reputable directories, such as Google My Business, Yelp, and industry-specific directories, strengthen your brand's authority. Citations are particularly important for local SEO, as they help search engines associate your brand with a specific location, improving the likelihood that you'll appear in local search results.

- **How to Build and Optimize Citations**: Start by ensuring your business information (name, address, phone number) is consistent across all platforms. Submit your business to reputable directories, review sites, and local listings, and regularly audit these sources for accuracy. For example, a local restaurant should make sure its name, address, and phone number (NAP) are consistently listed across sites like Yelp, TripAdvisor, and Google My Business. This consistency reassures search engines of your business's reliability and location.

Bringing It All Together: Leveraging Brand Mentions for SEO Success

Unlinked mentions and citations enhance your brand's visibility, credibility, and authority without relying solely on traditional backlinks. Both types of mentions provide valuable signals that support search engines' understanding of your brand's relevance, trustworthiness, and influence within your industry. Together, they reinforce your off-page SEO by positioning your brand as a recognized and respected entity.

C. Technical SEO Factors

1. Site Speed and Performance

Site speed and performance are crucial components of technical SEO, directly impacting user experience and search rankings. Page load times and Core Web Vitals are primary measures of site performance, with search engines like Google increasingly prioritizing fast, efficient websites in search results. A well-optimized, fast-loading website not only helps improve rankings but also reduces bounce rates and enhances user satisfaction, making it a critical area of focus for SEO.

Page Load Times: Enhancing User Experience and Reducing Bounce Rates

Page load time refers to how long it takes for a webpage to fully display on a user's screen. Faster load times contribute to a seamless user experience, while slow-loading pages can frustrate visitors and lead them to leave the site prematurely. Research shows that a page load time exceeding just a few seconds can significantly increase bounce rates, underscoring the importance of optimizing for speed.

- **Why Page Load Times Matter:** Search engines prioritize user satisfaction, and slow load times are a leading cause of poor user experience. Pages that load quickly are more likely to rank higher, as Google's algorithm favors sites that deliver content promptly. Additionally, users are more likely to stay and explore if pages load swiftly, which lowers bounce rates and increases engagement.

- **How to Improve Page Load Times:** Optimize images by compressing files without sacrificing quality, and leverage lazy loading for images and videos that are below the fold. Minify CSS, JavaScript, and HTML files to reduce file sizes and improve load times. Additionally, consider using a Content Delivery Network (CDN) to distribute site content across multiple servers, reducing latency for users in different geographic locations. For instance, an e-commerce site with high-resolution product images should ensure images are optimized to maintain visual quality while loading quickly.

Core Web Vitals: Meeting Google's Standards

Core Web Vitals are a set of performance metrics introduced by Google to assess a site's user experience. These metrics measure key aspects of site performance, including loading speed, interactivity, and visual stability. Optimizing Core Web Vitals is essential for SEO, as Google uses them as a ranking factor, rewarding sites that offer a smooth, responsive experience.

- **The Three Core Web Vitals:**
    - Largest Contentful Paint (LCP): Measures loading performance, focusing on the time it takes for the main content to load. Google recommenda a LCP is 2.5 seconds or faster.
    - First Input Delay (FID): Measures interactivity, or how quickly a page responds to user input. Google recommends the FID is less than 100 milliseconds.
    - Cumulative Layout Shift (CLS): Measures visual stability, tracking unexpected shifts in layout as the page loads. Google recommends a CLS score of less than 0.1.

- **Why Core Web Vitals Matter:** Core Web Vitals reflect how users experience a website, making them essential for ranking. Sites that meet or exceed Google's benchmarks are more likely to rank highly, as they provide a smoother, more reliable user experience. Optimizing for these metrics improves both performance and satisfaction.

- **How to Optimize Core Web Vitals:**
    - For LCP, focus on optimizing the main elements

that load first, such as large images, hero sections, and banners. Use faster servers, enable compression, and preload important resources to reduce loading times.
- For FID, minimize JavaScript execution to improve responsiveness. Deferring or delaying non-essential scripts can significantly reduce the time it takes for a page to become interactive.
- For CLS, ensure that elements on the page load predictably. Specify size attributes for images and ads to avoid unexpected shifts, and avoid inserting new content above existing elements as the page loads.

Bringing It All Together: Achieving Optimal Site Speed and Performance

Optimizing site speed and Core Web Vitals is fundamental to providing a high-quality user experience and improving SEO performance. By reducing page load times and meeting Google's Core Web Vitals benchmarks, you're creating a site that's both efficient and user-friendly—qualities that search engines prioritize. Faster sites with stable, responsive designs not only rank better but also retain visitors, leading to increased engagement and conversions.

2. Mobile-Friendliness

Mobile-friendliness is essential for SEO success. More than half of global web traffic comes from mobile devices, and search engines prioritize websites that deliver a seamless mobile experience. Mobile-friendliness involves two primary components: *responsive design* and *mobile-first indexing*. Optimizing your site for mobile users not only improves search rankings but also enhances user satisfaction, engagement, and accessibility.

Responsive Design: Ensuring a Seamless Experience Across All Devices

Responsive design is an approach that enables a website to adapt its layout and functionality based on the user's device, whether it's a desktop, tablet, or mobile phone. By using responsive design, websites can provide a consistent and user-friendly experience across all screen sizes, allowing content to display optimally without the need for separate mobile and desktop versions.

- **Why Responsive Design Matters**: Responsive design enhances user experience by providing a layout that's easy to navigate on any device. Websites that aren't responsive often force users to zoom, scroll excessively, or deal with broken layouts, leading to a frustrating experience. Search engines recognize these usability issues, and responsive design has become a significant ranking factor as it directly impacts user engagement and satisfaction.

- **How to Implement Responsive Design**: Use flexible grids, images, and CSS media queries to create a layout that adapts to different screen sizes. Test your site across a variety of devices and orientations to ensure that text, images, and interactive elements remain accessible and functional. For instance, on mobile devices, a responsive layout might feature larger buttons, a simplified menu, and vertically stacked content to make navigation easier. Tools like Google's Mobile-Friendly Test can help assess how well your site performs on mobile devices and highlight areas for improvement.

Mobile-First Indexing: Prioritizing the Mobile Version of Your Site

Google introduced mobile-first indexing in response to the growing number of mobile users, meaning that Google now predominantly uses the mobile version of a website for indexing and ranking. This change means that if a site is not optimized for mobile, it may not perform well in search results, even if the desktop version is well-optimized. Mobile-first indexing requires businesses to prioritize their mobile site performance and ensure that mobile and desktop versions provide consistent information.

- **Why Mobile-First Indexing Matters**: With mobile-first indexing, Google evaluates the mobile version of your site as the primary source of information, impacting both desktop and mobile search rankings. If your mobile site is incomplete or offers a diminished user experience, it could harm your overall SEO performance. Consistent content, metadata, and structured data across both versions are essential to ensure that your site ranks well.

- **How to Optimize for Mobile-First Indexing**: Start by ensuring that your mobile site includes all the content, images, and structured data present on your desktop site. Avoid hiding critical information on mobile to make the layout simpler; instead, use responsive design to ensure everything is accessible. Page speed is also crucial on mobile, so consider using Accelerated Mobile Pages (AMP) for faster load times. Regularly test your mobile site's usability, and use Google Search Console to monitor performance and detect any mobile-specific issues.

Bringing It All Together: Achieving a Mobile-Friendly Site for Improved SEO

Mobile-friendliness is a non-negotiable factor in modern SEO, as it directly affects both rankings and user experience. By implementing responsive design, you ensure that users across all devices can easily navigate and interact with your content. With mobile-first indexing, optimizing the mobile version of your site becomes paramount to your overall search performance. A mobile-friendly site not only ranks better but also fosters a more satisfying and engaging experience for users, encouraging them to stay longer and interact with your content.

3. Site Architecture and Navigation

A well-organized site architecture and clear navigation are essential for both user experience and SEO. Effective site structure helps search engines understand the relationships between pages, while intuitive navigation allows users to easily explore your content. Key elements of site architecture, such as URL structure, breadcrumbs, and sitemaps, play an important role in guiding search engine crawlers and enhancing the user journey.

URL Structure: Creating Descriptive and User-Friendly URLs

URL structure refers to the format and organization of URLs across your site. A clean, descriptive URL structure improves SEO by making it easier for both users and search engines to understand the content of each page. URLs that are short, keyword-rich, and well-organized contribute to better indexing and a more organized site.

- **Why URL Structure Matters**: Search engines use URLs to determine a page's topic and relevance. Descriptive URLs help search engines categorize your content accurately, improving visibility in search results. Additionally, user-friendly URLs that reflect the page's content help users understand what to expect before they click, which can increase click-through rates.

- **How to Optimize URL Structure**: Keep URLs short, meaningful, and aligned with your page titles. Use hyphens to separate words (e.g., "example.com/digital-marketing-tips") and include primary keywords relevant to each page. Avoid using numbers, special characters, or overly complex URL strings. Organize URLs in a logical hierarchy based on your site's structure; for instance, an e-commerce site could use "example.com/products/women/shoes" to reflect its categories.

Breadcrumbs: Improving Navigation and Search Visibility

Breadcrumbs are a secondary navigation system that shows users their location within the site's structure. Typically displayed at the top of a page, breadcrumbs provide a clickable trail back to higher-level pages, improving user experience and helping search engines understand the relationship between pages.

- **Why Breadcrumbs Matter**: Breadcrumbs make navigation easier, especially on larger websites with multiple levels of content. For search engines, breadcrumbs establish a clear content hierarchy, helping them index pages more effectively. Google often displays breadcrumb trails in search results, which can improve the visibility of your content and give users a better sense of the page structure.

- **How to Implement Breadcrumbs**: Use breadcrumb navigation that reflects your site's structure, ensuring that each breadcrumb in the trail is clickable. For example, a blog post on "Running Shoes" might display breadcrumbs as "Home > Products > Sportswear > Running Shoes." Breadcrumbs should follow a consistent format throughout the site. Implement structured data (Schema markup) for breadcrumbs to help search engines display them correctly in search results.

Sitemaps: Guiding Search Engine Crawlers

Sitemaps are files that list the URLs on your website, helping search engines discover and index your pages more efficiently. There are two primary types of sitemaps: *XML sitemaps* for search engines and *HTML sitemaps* for users. XML sitemaps inform search engines of your site's structure and provide metadata, such as the date a page was last updated, its importance, and how frequently it changes. HTML sitemaps, meanwhile, are user-facing and help visitors find important pages on your site.

- **Why Sitemaps Matter**: Sitemaps ensure that search engines can access and crawl your entire site, even if some pages are not linked from the main navigation. This is especially useful for large sites, e-commerce sites with multiple product categories, or sites with frequently updated content. A well-organized sitemap increases the chances that all pages will be indexed and ranked, ultimately improving search visibility.

- **How to Create and Optimize Sitemaps**:
    - **XML Sitemap**: Use an SEO tool or plugin to generate an XML sitemap that automatically updates as you add new content. Include all essential URLs, and submit the sitemap to Google Search Console and Bing Webmaster

Tools to ensure search engines have access to the latest version.
- **HTML Sitemap**: Create an HTML sitemap that links to key pages, organized in a way that users can easily understand. This serves as a navigation aid, particularly for users who are trying to find specific information quickly. Link to the HTML sitemap in your site's footer.

Bringing It All Together: Building a Solid Site Architecture

A strong site architecture, with optimized URL structures, breadcrumbs, and sitemaps, creates a solid foundation for SEO and user experience. Clear URLs make it easy for both users and search engines to understand your content, while breadcrumbs and sitemaps enhance navigation and crawling efficiency. By organizing your site with these elements in mind, you're making it easier for search engines to index your pages, which ultimately improves your search visibility and rankings.

4. Security

Website security is a fundamental aspect of technical SEO, directly affecting user trust and search rankings. In an age where data privacy and online safety are paramount, search engines prioritize sites that demonstrate a commitment to protecting user information. Two critical components of website security for SEO are *HTTPS encryption* and *safe browsing*. By implementing these security measures, you not only enhance user trust but also improve your site's chances of ranking well in search results.

HTTPS Encryption: Protecting User Data and Boosting SEO

HTTPS (Hypertext Transfer Protocol Secure) is a secure version of HTTP, which encrypts data exchanged between a user's browser and your website. HTTPS ensures that sensitive information, such as login credentials and payment details, is transmitted securely, protecting it from potential interception by malicious parties. Beyond data security, HTTPS has become an SEO ranking factor, with Google and other search engines prioritizing sites with HTTPS encryption over non-secure sites.

- **Why HTTPS Encryption Matters**: In addition to protecting user data, HTTPS signals to users and search engines that your site is trustworthy and legitimate. Google has explicitly stated that HTTPS is a ranking factor, and non-secure sites (HTTP) are often labeled with a "Not Secure" warning in browsers, which can deter users from proceeding. Sites with HTTPS encryption are more likely to rank higher and retain user trust.

- **How to Implement HTTPS**: To enable HTTPS on your site, obtain an SSL (Secure Sockets Layer) certificate from a trusted certificate authority (CA). Many web hosts offer SSL certificates, often included in their hosting plans. Once installed, update all internal links and references to ensure they use HTTPS. Regularly renew the SSL certificate and monitor for any mixed content issues (when some elements on a page are loaded via HTTP), as they can undermine your site's security and user trust.

Safe Browsing: Preventing Malware and Phishing Threats

Safe browsing refers to Google's initiative to protect users from potentially harmful content, including malware, phishing, and deceptive practices. Sites that expose users to security risks may be flagged with warnings, reducing trust and making it less likely for users to proceed. Safe browsing helps ensure that users can explore your site safely, and search engines prioritize sites that adhere to these security standards.

- **Why Safe Browsing Matters**: Search engines, particularly Google, penalize sites that pose a risk to users. If your site is flagged for unsafe content, search engines may display a warning to users before they enter, negatively affecting traffic, user engagement, and rankings. Maintaining a safe browsing environment is essential not only for SEO but also for protecting your reputation and user trust.

- **How to Maintain Safe Browsing**: Regularly monitor your site for potential security threats, such as malware, outdated software, and vulnerable plugins. Use security tools, like Google Search Console's Security Issues report, to identify and address risks. Implement firewall protection, use reputable plugins and themes, and regularly update all site software to mitigate vulnerabilities. If your site is ever flagged, address the issues promptly and request a review in Google Search Console to remove the warning.

Bringing It All Together: Building a Secure Foundation for SEO

Security measures like HTTPS encryption and safe browsing are essential to a successful SEO strategy. By securing user data with HTTPS and maintaining a safe browsing environment, you're not only protecting visitors but also boosting your site's credibility and search engine rankings. These security enhancements contribute to a more reliable and trustworthy user experience, which aligns with the values of both search engines and users.

D. User-Specific Factors

1. Location Data

Location data is a key element in SEO for businesses seeking to attract local customers. Optimizing for location-specific searches involves two primary components: *Local SEO* and *Geo-Targeting*. These strategies enable businesses to appear in search results for users in specific geographic areas, making it easier to connect with nearby audiences. By implementing location-based SEO tactics, businesses can improve their visibility in local search results, drive foot traffic, and build a stronger presence within their community.

Local SEO: Optimizing for Local Search Visibility

Local SEO is the practice of optimizing your online presence to attract business from local searches. This is especially important for businesses with physical locations or those that serve specific regions. Local SEO helps your business appear in local search results, such as Google's Local Pack, and ensures that nearby users find accurate and relevant information about your business when searching for services in their area.

- **Why Local SEO Matters**: Local SEO is essential for businesses that depend on foot traffic or local customers, as it drives more targeted, qualified leads. According to Google, nearly half of all searches have local intent, such as users looking for "restaurants near me" or "plumbers in [city]." Optimizing for local SEO can significantly improve visibility and increase the likelihood of appearing in these searches.

- **How to Optimize for Local SEO**: Start by claiming

and optimizing your Google My Business (GMB) listing, which allows your business to appear in Google's Local Pack. Ensure that your GMB profile is complete and accurate, including your address, hours of operation, contact information, and photos. Encourage customers to leave reviews, as positive ratings can boost your ranking in local search results. Additionally, use local keywords in your content, such as city or neighborhood names, and create location-based landing pages if you have multiple locations (e.g., "Denver Coffee Shop" or "Plumbing Services in Austin").

Geo-Targeting: Reaching Users Based on Their Location

Geo-targeting is a strategy that involves delivering content or ads based on the user's geographic location. Unlike general local SEO, which improves search visibility for a business in a specific location, geo-targeting tailors content and messaging to users based on their location. This tactic is especially useful for digital marketing campaigns aimed at specific regions, cities, or neighborhoods.

- **Why Geo-Targeting Matters**: Geo-targeting allows businesses to provide more relevant and personalized information to users based on their location, improving the effectiveness of marketing efforts. By aligning content with the user's immediate needs and environment, geo-targeting can drive higher engagement and conversions. For instance, a clothing retailer might promote winter wear to users in colder climates, while showing summer apparel to users in warmer areas.

- **How to Implement Geo-Targeting**: Use geo-targeting features in platforms like Google Ads or Facebook Ads to display ads to users in specific locations. On your website, consider creating dynamic content that adapts to the user's location, such as offering store-specific promotions or showing location-based product availability. Additionally, leverage location-based keywords on your website to increase relevance in location-specific searches, like "Best Mexican Restaurant in Chicago" or "Electricians near Brooklyn."

Bringing It All Together: Leveraging Location Data for SEO Success

Location data is a powerful tool for connecting with local audiences and enhancing your presence in specific areas. By implementing Local SEO and geo-targeting strategies, you make your business more accessible and relevant to users in your target region, increasing your chances of appearing in local searches. These strategies enable you to drive more targeted traffic, build stronger relationships with nearby customers, and position your brand as a go-to resource within the community.

2. Search History and Personalization

Personalization in search results is an important factor in modern SEO, as search engines like Google use search history and past user behavior to deliver tailored results. This personalized approach helps search engines understand individual preferences and anticipate needs, making search results more relevant to each user. For businesses, understanding how search history and personalization work can enhance content strategy and user engagement by aligning with personalized search trends.

Tailored Results: Leveraging Search History to Enhance Relevance

Search engines use search history and interaction data to deliver results that align closely with a user's past behavior and preferences. When users regularly search for certain topics or frequently visit specific types of websites, search engines adjust future search results to reflect these patterns, delivering content that is likely to be relevant based on the user's established interests.

- **Why Tailored Results Matter**: Tailored results improve user satisfaction by making it easier for users to find what they're looking. For SEO, this means that if a user has engaged with your brand or similar brands before, your content has a higher chance of appearing in that user's personalized search results. Personalization can increase the likelihood of users returning to your site, boosting engagement, brand loyalty, and long-term traffic.

- **How to Optimize for Tailored Results**: To benefit from personalized search, focus on delivering consistent, high-quality content that builds user trust and encourages return visits. Engage users across multiple channels, such as email newsletters and social media, to stay top of mind. Implement retargeting strategies to reach users who have previously visited your site, reinforcing brand familiarity and encouraging repeat engagement. For instance, if a user frequently visits your blog on fitness tips, offering personalized recommendations for related articles or products can keep them engaged and improve their overall experience with your brand.

Personalization: Aligning Content with User Preferences

Personalization goes beyond search history by tailoring content to individual user preferences and behaviors. Search engines can personalize results based on factors like location, device, language settings, and browsing history, delivering customized results that reflect what's most relevant for each user. Personalization has made search more dynamic and adaptive, creating opportunities for businesses to reach users with highly targeted content.

- **Why Personalization Matters**: Personalized results foster a better user experience by prioritizing content that resonates with users' needs and interests. For SEO, this presents an opportunity to capture long-term engagement by delivering content that matches users' unique preferences. Users who consistently see relevant results from your brand are more likely to return, explore further, and engage more deeply with your content.

- **How to Implement Personalization in Content Strategy**: Develop content that addresses a wide range of topics within your niche to appeal to diverse user interests. Use data analytics to understand what content performs well with specific segments of your audience and tailor your future content accordingly. On your website, consider dynamic content strategies, such as recommended products or personalized blog posts based on users' past interactions. For example, an e-commerce site can offer personalized product recommendations based on previous purchases or browsing behavior, increasing the likelihood of conversions.

Bringing It All Together: Optimizing for Search History and Personalization

Personalization and search history play a crucial role in modern SEO, allowing search engines to connect users with content that best aligns with their past behavior and preferences. By focusing on consistent, high-quality content and leveraging personalized engagement tactics, you can strengthen your brand's connection with users and increase the likelihood of appearing in their customized search results.

3. Device and Platform

In the era of multi-device internet usage, optimizing for different devices and platforms is essential for SEO success. Users access websites on desktops, laptops, tablets, and mobile phones, each with unique screen sizes, performance capabilities, and browsing preferences. Ensuring that your site performs seamlessly across devices and is compatible with various browsers improves user experience and helps search engines prioritize your content in search rankings. This involves two key aspects: *Desktop vs. Mobile Optimization* and *Browser Compatibility*.

Desktop vs. Mobile: Adapting to User Preferences and Mobile-First Indexing

Desktop and mobile optimization involve tailoring your site's design, layout, and functionality to ensure smooth performance on both large and small screens. With Google's mobile-first indexing, the mobile version of your website is now the primary version used for indexing and ranking. This makes mobile optimization crucial, especially as more users rely on mobile devices to browse the internet.

- **Why Desktop vs. Mobile Optimization Matters**: Mobile traffic accounts for a large percentage of overall web traffic, making a mobile-friendly site essential for user engagement and SEO. Mobile-first indexing means that if your mobile site is poorly optimized, it could negatively impact your rankings on all devices, not just mobile. Optimizing for both desktop and mobile ensures a cohesive user experience and maintains your site's accessibility and usability across device types.

- **How to Optimize for Desktop and Mobile**: Use responsive design to create a site layout that automatically adapts to different screen sizes. On mobile, prioritize fast load times, touch-friendly navigation, and concise content to enhance usability. Test interactive elements, such as buttons and menus, to ensure they work well on smaller screens. Additionally, optimize images and videos to prevent slow loading on mobile devices. For example, an e-commerce site might simplify its layout on mobile, using larger buttons, a clean product gallery, and streamlined navigation. Tools like Google's Mobile-Friendly Test can help evaluate mobile performance and highlight areas for improvement.

Browser Compatibility: Ensuring a Consistent Experience Across Browsers

Browser compatibility refers to the ability of your website to function and display correctly across different web browsers, including Chrome, Safari, Firefox, and Edge. Each browser has its own rendering engine and can interpret code slightly differently, meaning a site that looks perfect on Chrome might appear broken or load improperly on another browser. Ensuring compatibility across browsers is essential for providing a consistent user experience and maximizing accessibility.

- **Why Browser Compatibility Matters**: Users access websites on a wide range of browsers, and a lack of compatibility can lead to a poor experience for a portion of your audience. Inconsistent display, broken elements, or slow loading times on certain browsers can lead to higher bounce rates and reduced engagement, impacting SEO. By ensuring your site is compatible across major browsers, you avoid alienating users and maintain a unified experience.

- **How to Achieve Browser Compatibility**: Test your site on all major browsers to ensure it displays correctly and functions as intended. Use cross-browser testing tools like BrowserStack or CrossBrowserTesting to identify compatibility issues and address them proactively. Follow web standards and best practices in coding (e.g., using HTML5 and CSS3) to improve consistency across browsers. For instance, certain CSS features may render differently in older versions of Internet Explorer, so avoid relying on non-standard CSS properties. Additionally, test interactive elements, videos, and scripts to verify that they load and function across browsers without glitches.

Bringing It All Together: Optimizing for Device and Platform Compatibility

Device and platform compatibility is crucial for delivering a high-quality user experience across desktop and mobile devices as well as various browsers. By implementing responsive design and optimizing for mobile-first indexing, you ensure your site performs well on both large and small screens. Additionally, by maintaining browser compatibility, you create a unified experience that meets users' expectations, no matter which browser they use.

E. The Interplay of Ranking Factors

SEO success relies on a complex web of ranking factors that don't operate in isolation; they influence and reinforce each other to determine how well a page performs in search results. A cohesive SEO strategy requires an understanding of how these factors interact, as optimizing one area can have a ripple effect across other aspects of site performance and visibility. Let's explore how key factors—such as content quality, user engagement, technical SEO, and off-page SEO—work together to improve rankings and user experience.

1. How Factors Influence Each Other

A. Content Quality and User Engagement: Building Relevance and Authority

Content quality is central to SEO, but even the most valuable content can struggle to rank if it doesn't engage users effectively. High-quality content that's original, in-depth, and relevant encourages longer time on page, lower bounce rates, and increased interaction—key engagement metrics that search engines monitor as indicators of user satisfaction. When users engage deeply with content, search engines recognize this as a signal of relevance, which can improve rankings.

- **Example**: Suppose a blog post on "Healthy Meal Prep Tips" provides well-researched information and actionable steps. If it's engaging, users will spend more time reading it, may share it on social media, and are likely to explore related content. This engagement positively reinforces the content's quality in the eyes of search engines, boosting its authority and relevance for similar search queries.

B. Technical SEO and User Experience: Supporting Accessibility and Performance

Technical SEO elements like site speed, mobile-friendliness, and secure browsing directly affect user experience, influencing how users interact with your site and, consequently, your rankings. Fast load times, responsive design, and secure HTTPS encryption create a smooth, reliable experience that encourages users to stay longer and interact with your content. These technical optimizations, in turn, impact engagement metrics, which play a role in ranking decisions.

- **Example**: A website optimized for mobile with fast load times and clear navigation will retain more users and reduce bounce rates. When users can quickly find what they need without delays, they are more likely to engage further with the site. Search engines interpret this positive experience as a sign of a high-quality site, reinforcing its ranking potential.

C. Off-Page SEO and Authority: Boosting Credibility and Visibility

Off-page SEO factors, like backlinks and brand mentions, build a site's authority and reputation, signaling to search engines that the site is a trusted source of information. Quality backlinks from authoritative sites amplify content credibility, and when combined with strong on-page content and positive engagement, they can propel rankings even higher. Conversely, if a site has a weak backlink profile, its ranking may suffer despite strong on-page content.

- **Example**: If a page on "Sustainable Fashion Trends" earns backlinks from reputable fashion blogs and sustainability publications, search engines view this as an endorsement of the content's credibility. This off-page authority boosts the ranking potential of the page, especially when paired with high-quality content and positive engagement metrics.

D. Keyword Optimization and Content Structure: Enhancing Relevance and Discoverability

Effective keyword optimization, combined with well-organized content structure, makes it easier for search engines to understand the content's relevance to specific queries. Using primary keywords, LSI keywords, and related terms naturally within a structured format improves both on-page SEO and user experience. Proper use of headers, internal links, and meta tags further supports discoverability, encouraging search engines to index and rank the content more effectively.

- **Example**: A page optimized for the keyword "Best Plant-Based Diet Recipes" with a clear, organized structure that includes subtopics like "High-Protein Plant-Based Meals" and "Easy Vegan Snacks" makes it easier for users to navigate and find relevant information. The use of related keywords within the content helps search engines understand its full context, which can improve rankings for a range of related search queries.

E. Social Signals and Engagement: Amplifying Reach and Authority

Social signals, such as shares, likes, and comments, help content reach a broader audience and generate engagement that can indirectly boost rankings. When content is widely shared, it not only increases traffic but also has the potential to attract natural backlinks from other websites, further enhancing authority. Social engagement also signals to search engines that content resonates with audiences, which can positively influence rankings.

- **Example**: A guide on "Tips for First-Time Home Buyers" that garners significant social engagement on platforms like Facebook or LinkedIn may attract more visitors and social proof. The increased exposure can lead to more backlinks, which, combined with high engagement metrics, strengthen the content's authority and relevance for related search queries.

Bringing It All Together: The Holistic Impact of SEO Factors

The interplay of SEO ranking factors demonstrates that a successful strategy involves balance and integration. High-quality content enhances user engagement, technical SEO supports accessibility, off-page SEO builds authority, and social signals extend reach—all of which work together to strengthen overall performance. When these factors are aligned, they reinforce each other, creating a comprehensive approach that improves rankings, user satisfaction, and long-term visibility.

2. Prioritizing Factors for Maximum Impact

With a multitude of ranking factors in play, it's crucial to prioritize the ones that will deliver the most substantial impact on your SEO goals. Some factors, like content quality and site performance, have a broad influence and should be prioritized universally, while others, such as local SEO or social signals, may vary in importance depending on your audience, industry, and business objectives. By focusing on high-impact factors first, you can maximize your return on SEO efforts and build a strong foundation for long-term success.

A. Content Quality and Relevance: The Cornerstone of SEO

Content quality is consistently a top priority in SEO because it directly influences user engagement, relevance, and authority. Well-researched, valuable, and user-centered content not only ranks well but also keeps users engaged, drives shares, and attracts backlinks. Prioritizing content quality ensures that all other SEO efforts are supporting a strong base, making it easier to drive traffic, engagement, and credibility.

- **Key Actions**: Invest in creating comprehensive, high-value content tailored to user intent. Use keyword research to align content topics with what users are searching for, and incorporate relevant keywords and LSI terms naturally throughout. Focus on depth, originality, and user satisfaction, and ensure that each piece of content delivers real value to the audience.

B. Technical SEO: Ensuring Site Accessibility and Performance

Technical SEO plays a foundational role by ensuring that search engines can efficiently crawl, index, and understand your content. Factors like page speed, mobile-friendliness, and site security have a direct impact on rankings and user experience. Optimizing technical SEO helps eliminate barriers to discovery and enhances the accessibility and usability of your site, making it a high-priority area for maximum impact.

- **Key Actions**: Start by implementing HTTPS for security and optimizing page load times, particularly on mobile. Use tools like Google's PageSpeed Insights to identify performance bottlenecks, and apply responsive design to improve mobile usability. Conduct regular technical audits to ensure all pages are accessible to search engine crawlers, and submit an updated XML sitemap to facilitate indexing.

C. User Engagement Metrics: Focusing on Behavior and Satisfaction

User engagement metrics like bounce rate, time on page, and click-through rate (CTR) indicate how well your content meets user expectations. Search engines interpret these metrics as indicators of content relevance and quality. Prioritizing engagement metrics not only helps improve rankings but also fosters a more meaningful connection with your audience, encouraging users to stay longer and explore more content.

- **Key Actions**: Optimize content for readability and user experience by using clear headings, concise paragraphs, and engaging multimedia. Test and refine your titles and meta descriptions to boost CTR, and use internal linking to guide users to related content. Monitoring user behavior through analytics tools allows you to identify areas for improvement and continuously enhance user satisfaction.

D. Mobile-Friendliness and Core Web Vitals: Enhancing Mobile Experience

With Google's mobile-first indexing and the growing trend of mobile usage, mobile-friendliness has become a priority factor. Core Web Vitals—metrics that measure page load speed, interactivity, and visual stability—also play a crucial role in SEO, as they affect both rankings and user experience on mobile and desktop. By prioritizing mobile usability and Core Web Vitals, you make your site more accessible to users on all devices, improving rankings and engagement.

- **Key Actions**: Focus on achieving optimal scores for Core Web Vitals: Largest Contentful Paint (LCP), First Input Delay (FID), and Cumulative Layout Shift (CLS). Use responsive design principles to ensure a consistent experience across devices, and optimize for fast loading times by compressing images and minifying code. Testing your site on various devices and screen sizes helps identify and resolve mobile usability issues.

E. Backlink Quality: Building Authority and Credibility

High-quality backlinks from reputable websites significantly enhance a site's authority, signaling to search engines that your content is valuable and trustworthy. Backlinks are among the most influential off-page SEO factors, and prioritizing quality over quantity is essential. A few authoritative links from respected sources can have a more substantial impact than numerous links from low-quality sites.

- **Key Actions**: Focus on acquiring backlinks through organic, high-quality content that naturally attracts attention. Engage in guest posting on industry-relevant sites, develop relationships with influencers, and participate in industry collaborations to gain exposure. Monitor your backlink profile for low-quality or spammy links, and disavow any that could harm your site's reputation.

F. Local SEO (If Applicable): Capturing Nearby Audiences

For businesses with physical locations or those that rely on local customers, local SEO should be a top priority. Optimizing for local search improves visibility in geographic-specific searches and drives targeted traffic to your site. This involves focusing on factors like Google My Business (GMB) optimization, local keywords, and reviews.

- **Key Actions**: Claim and optimize your GMB listing with accurate, up-to-date information, and encourage customers to leave positive reviews. Use local keywords in your content and on key landing pages to capture geographically targeted searches. Additionally, submit your business information to local directories for improved local search visibility.

G. Social Signals (For Content Visibility and Brand Awareness)

While social signals like shares, likes, and comments aren't direct ranking factors, they amplify content reach and visibility. Strong social engagement can drive traffic to your site, attract natural backlinks, and build brand awareness. For businesses seeking to increase exposure, social media can be a powerful complement to traditional SEO efforts.

- **Key Actions**: Share high-value content across your social media platforms and encourage user engagement through questions, polls, or discussions. Make it easy for users to share your content by including social sharing buttons on your website. Monitoring social performance allows you to refine your strategy and focus on the platforms where your audience is most active.

Bringing It All Together: A Balanced Approach to SEO Prioritization

Prioritizing these factors allows you to build a well-rounded SEO strategy that maximizes impact by focusing on high-value areas first. By strengthening content quality, technical SEO, and user engagement, you create a strong foundation that supports other optimizations, such as mobile-friendliness, backlink acquisition, and local SEO. A balanced, prioritized approach enables you to drive meaningful results, enhance user experience, and continually adapt.

Chapter 4. The Logic Behind Search Engine Operations

Understanding the logic behind search engine operations is key to unlocking effective SEO strategies. Search engines are designed to connect users with the most relevant, high-quality content, and they do this by interpreting signals from hundreds of factors. At the heart of search engine functionality are algorithms that evaluate user intent, content relevance, site authority, and user experience. By grasping the principles that guide these algorithms—such as understanding user intent, prioritizing content quality, and analyzing engagement metrics—SEO practitioners can better align their strategies with search engine goals.

A. Understanding User Intent

User intent is the goal or purpose behind a search query. Search engines use advanced algorithms and AI to analyze query patterns, user behavior, and contextual clues to determine what users truly want to find. Broadly, user intent can be classified into three main categories: navigational, informational, and transactional queries. Each category requires a unique SEO approach to effectively meet user needs and improve search engine rankings.

- **Navigational Queries**: These searches are conducted when users have a specific destination in mind, such as a website or a particular page. For example, a user searching for "Facebook login" is looking to navigate directly to Facebook's login page. Navigational queries often reflect brand-driven intent and can indicate user loyalty or preference for a specific company or product. For SEO, this means ensuring your brand's pages are easy to locate and optimized for branded keywords.

- **Informational Queries**: Informational searches are used when users seek answers, insights, or explanations. Examples include "how to cook pasta" or "what is SEO." These searches are typically broad and focus on learning rather than making a purchase or reaching a specific page. To capture traffic from informational queries, SEO strategies should focus on high-quality, informative content that directly addresses user questions. Content like blog posts, tutorials, FAQs, and educational articles is effective here, as it provides value and positions your site as an authority on the topic.

- **Transactional Queries**: Transactional queries indicate a user's intent to make a purchase or take a specific action, such as downloading an app or signing up for a newsletter. Examples include searches like "buy running shoes online" or "best deals on laptops." Transactional intent is closely linked to conversions, so content optimized for these queries should have a clear call-to-action and facilitate the user's journey from search to purchase. Product pages, e-commerce listings, and conversion-focused landing pages are essential for targeting transactional queries, and these pages should include keyword-rich descriptions, customer reviews, and relevant calls to action.

By understanding and catering to these different types of user intent, SEO professionals can create content that not only satisfies user expectations but also aligns with the algorithms that drive search engine rankings. Recognizing user intent helps improve relevance, enhances user experience, and ultimately leads to higher engagement and conversion rates.

B. The Importance of Relevance and Authority

Relevance and authority are two foundational pillars in how search engines evaluate content, helping them determine which pages are most likely to satisfy a user's query. Relevance refers to how closely a page's content matches the search intent, while authority gauges the credibility and trustworthiness of that content. Search engines like Google use sophisticated algorithms to assess these qualities, prioritizing content that is both relevant to the user's search and from a reliable source. Understanding how relevance and authority impact search rankings allows SEO practitioners to craft content that resonates with both users and algorithms, boosting visibility and credibility.

1. Relevance: Aligning Content with User Intent

Relevance is the measure of how well a page's content aligns with the intent behind a user's search query. Search engines analyze multiple elements to determine relevance, including keywords, content structure, and user engagement metrics. The goal is to surface pages that not only match the keywords entered but also fulfill the specific needs or intentions of the searcher—whether they're seeking information, navigating to a specific site, or making a purchase.

- **How Search Engines Determine Relevance**: Algorithms assess relevance by examining keywords in the title, meta description, headers, and body of the content. However, modern search engines go beyond keywords, employing Natural Language Processing (NLP) to understand context, synonyms, and user intent. For example, a search for "best coffee shops near me" prompts results with location-based and highly-rated coffee shop listings, showing that search engines understand the local and quality aspects of the query.

- **Optimizing for Relevance**: To improve relevance, focus on creating content that addresses specific user questions and needs. Conduct keyword research to identify phrases that reflect user intent and incorporate these naturally throughout your content. Additionally, use structured data and clear formatting to help search engines better interpret your content's purpose, making it more likely to appear for relevant queries.

2. Authority: Building Trustworthiness and Credibility

Authority is the measure of a website's credibility, determined by factors such as backlinks, brand mentions, and domain age. Search engines prioritize content from authoritative sources because it's perceived as more likely to provide accurate, valuable information. Pages with high authority are typically linked to by reputable sites, have a consistent online presence, and demonstrate expertise.

- **How Search Engines Determine Authority**: Authority is largely influenced by off-page factors, especially the quality and quantity of backlinks from other credible websites. Links from trusted sites act as endorsements, signaling that a page is a reliable resource. In addition to backlinks, search engines assess brand mentions, reviews, and the author's expertise to establish authority. For example, a health website that is frequently referenced by medical organizations and written by licensed professionals will be seen as more authoritative than a similar site without these endorsements.

- **Optimizing for Authority**: To build authority, focus on creating high-quality content that naturally attracts backlinks from reputable sites. Collaborate with industry influencers, guest post on credible platforms, and engage with trusted sites within your niche. Additionally, use an author bio section that highlights your expertise and credentials, helping search engines and users trust the content you're providing.

Bringing It All Together: Balancing Relevance and Authority for SEO Success

For content to perform well in search rankings, it must balance both relevance and authority. Relevant content answers users' questions and meets their needs, while authority signals that the information comes from a credible, trusted source. By focusing on both aspects, SEO practitioners can create content that satisfies search engine criteria, ultimately boosting visibility, engagement, and trust.

C. The Goal of User Satisfaction

At the core of search engine operations is a commitment to delivering the best possible experience for users. User satisfaction goes beyond simply providing relevant and authoritative content; it involves creating a seamless, engaging, and enjoyable journey from the moment users enter a search query to the completion of their task. Search engines prioritize pages that align with this goal, rewarding sites that provide high-quality, easy-to-navigate content that keeps users engaged. By focusing on user satisfaction, SEO practitioners can create content that not only ranks well but also resonates with audiences, fostering long-term engagement and trust.

1. User Experience (UX): Enhancing Engagement and Ease of Use

User experience is a critical aspect of user satisfaction and encompasses everything from site speed and mobile-friendliness to navigation and design. A well-designed user experience makes it easy for visitors to find what they're looking for, and keeps them engaged. Search engines use metrics like bounce rate, time on page, and click-through rate to evaluate UX, giving preference to sites that demonstrate strong engagement and smooth usability.

- **Why UX Matters:** A positive user experience encourages users to stay longer on your site, explore additional content, and ultimately complete their desired actions. Search engines interpret these behaviors as indicators of high-quality content, which can lead to improved rankings. Conversely, a poor UX—such as slow loading times or confusing navigation—can lead to higher bounce rates, signaling to search engines that the content may not be meeting user needs.

- **How to Optimize UX for SEO:** Prioritize fast loading times by optimizing images and reducing unnecessary code, as slow pages often lead to user drop-offs. Implement responsive design to ensure your site looks and functions well on both desktop and mobile devices. Use clear headings, intuitive menus, and concise content to help users find what they need quickly. Tools like Google's Core Web Vitals can help measure and improve UX factors that contribute to user satisfaction.

2. Content Quality: Meeting User Needs with Valuable Information

Content quality remains a central factor in user satisfaction, as users visit a site primarily to find answers, gain insights, or complete tasks. High-quality content is comprehensive, well-researched, and directly aligned with the user's search intent. By delivering value through helpful, actionable information, content that meets user needs enhances satisfaction and encourages repeat visits.

- **Why Content Quality Matters:** Search engines reward pages that provide value, as these pages are more likely to satisfy user intent. High-quality content not only improves engagement but also attracts backlinks and shares, further signaling authority to search engines. Additionally, users are more likely to trust and return to a site that consistently delivers relevant, accurate information.

- **How to Optimize Content for User Satisfaction:** Tailor content to the specific needs of your target audience by conducting keyword research to understand what they're searching for. Create comprehensive guides, answers to FAQs, and actionable insights that go beyond surface-level information. Format content for readability by using headings, bullet points, and visuals, which make it easier for users to scan and absorb the information.

3. Visual Appeal and Readability: Creating an Enjoyable Experience

Visual appeal and readability contribute to user satisfaction by making content engaging and accessible. A well-designed page with an appealing layout, clear fonts, and quality visuals enhances user experience and keeps users engaged. Readability is particularly important; content that is easy to read and understand reduces user frustration and improves information retention.

- **Why Visual Appeal and Readability Matter:** When users enjoy the visual experience of a site and find the content easy to read, they are more likely to stay engaged and explore additional pages. Search engines factor in engagement metrics as part of their ranking criteria, meaning a visually appealing, readable site can help improve SEO performance. High-quality visuals also increase shareability, potentially leading to more social signals and backlinks.

- **How to Enhance Visual Appeal and Readability:** Use a clean design with a consistent color scheme, clear fonts, and spacing that makes text easy to read. Break up long blocks of text with subheadings, images, and bullet points. High-quality visuals like infographics, videos, and images not only add aesthetic value but also help convey information in an engaging way. Additionally, consider implementing dark mode or larger text options for accessibility, further enhancing user satisfaction.

Bringing It All Together: Prioritizing User Satisfaction for SEO Success

User satisfaction is the ultimate goal of search engines, as it ensures that users receive a positive, relevant, and engaging experience. By focusing on user experience, content quality, and visual appeal, SEO practitioners can create a site that not only meets search engine criteria but also provides genuine value to audiences. This holistic approach to user satisfaction builds trust, encourages repeat visits, and strengthens brand loyalty, all of which contribute to improved search visibility and growth.

Chapter 5. AI-Driven Changes in Search

Artificial Intelligence (AI) is transforming the way search engines operate, leading to a more sophisticated and personalized search experience. With advancements in AI technologies like machine learning, natural language processing (NLP), and deep learning, search engines are now able to interpret complex queries, understand context, and anticipate user needs more accurately than ever before. These AI-driven changes have shifted the focus of SEO from simply optimizing for keywords to creating content that meets nuanced user intent, fosters engagement, and aligns with personalized search behaviors.

A. AI Technologies Shaping Search

AI has fundamentally altered the way search engines interpret and rank content, making the search process more sophisticated, personalized, and user-centric. Three key AI-driven technologies—*Natural Language Processing (NLP)*, *Machine Learning Algorithms*, and *AI Content Detection*—are at the forefront of this transformation. Each of these technologies plays a critical role in shaping search results, assessing content quality, and influencing SEO strategies. Let's explore how these technologies impact search and what it means for SEO.

1. Natural Language Processing (NLP): Understanding Context and Intent

Natural Language Processing (NLP) enables search engines to interpret the complexities of human language, including context, semantics, and user intent. NLP allows search engines to move beyond simple keyword matching and into understanding the deeper meaning behind user queries, enabling them to deliver results that better align with users' needs.

- **How NLP Works in Search**: NLP uses advanced algorithms to analyze language and context. Google's BERT (Bidirectional Encoder Representations from Transformers) algorithm, for instance, allows Google to process conversational queries and understand relationships between words that change the meaning of a search. With NLP, search engines can determine the intent behind queries like "how to prevent carpal tunnel in remote work" and deliver results specifically about preventive measures rather than general information about carpal tunnel syndrome.

- **Impact on SEO**: For SEO practitioners, optimizing for NLP requires focusing on content that addresses user intent comprehensively. Rather than relying solely on isolated keywords, it's important to create natural, informative content that answers specific user questions. Using related terms, variations, and question-based headings can improve the relevance of content for NLP-driven algorithms. Content that flows naturally and mimics conversational language is more likely to rank well, as it aligns with the search engine's improved understanding of context and nuance.

2. Machine Learning Algorithms: Continuous Learning and Personalization

Machine learning enables search engines to analyze user behavior, learn from it, and continuously refine search results to better meet user expectations. Unlike traditional algorithms with static rules, machine learning algorithms evolve based on real-time user interactions, making search results more dynamic and responsive to trends.

- **How Machine Learning Works in Search**: Machine learning analyzes patterns in data, using insights from user behavior (such as click-through rates, bounce rates, and time on page) to predict which results are most likely to satisfy a given query. Google's RankBrain, for example, is a machine learning component of its algorithm that learns from user engagement data. If users consistently interact with certain pages for a specific query, RankBrain learns to prioritize those pages for similar queries in the future. Machine learning is also responsible for personalization, tailoring results to individual preferences, search history, and location.

- **Impact on SEO**: Machine learning has made engagement metrics like dwell time and CTR crucial components of SEO. To optimize for machine learning, content should not only address user needs but also encourage interaction and engagement. Pages that keep users engaged and provide a positive experience are more likely to benefit from machine learning-driven algorithms. A/B testing content strategies, refining UX design, and regularly updating content based on performance analytics are effective ways to align with the adaptive nature of machine learning in search.

3. AI Content Detection: Evaluating Human-Centric vs. AI-Generated Content

As AI-generated content becomes more prevalent, search engines have introduced AI content detection algorithms to distinguish between human-generated and machine-generated content. While AI can be a valuable tool for content creation, search engines tend to prioritize content that reflects human understanding, creativity, and nuance, as this type of content is more likely to provide genuine value to users. As a result, content that is solely AI-generated may be ranked lower if it lacks the depth, originality, or human touch that enhances user satisfaction.

- **How AI Content Detection Works in Search**: AI content detection algorithms analyze factors like sentence structure, coherence, and originality to identify whether content is likely generated by AI or crafted by humans. Google's guidelines emphasize the importance of "helpful content," and recent updates have aimed at identifying and potentially downranking content that appears to be produced for search manipulation or lacks authentic value. AI detectors can recognize patterns typical of automated content, such as repetitive phrasing, lack of depth, and predictable sentence structures. Some detectors also evaluate the use of AI-generated images or videos as part of content quality assessment.

- **Impact on SEO**: For SEO professionals, it's essential to use AI as a supportive tool rather than a complete content generator. To avoid penalties or lower rankings, prioritize creating content that reflects human insight, expertise, and empathy. If AI is used in the content creation process, it's advisable to edit and refine the output to add depth, creativity, and context. Combining human input with AI can enhance content without sacrificing authenticity, helping it align with search engines' emphasis on high-quality, user-focused material.

Bringing It All Together: Adapting SEO Strategies to AI-Driven Search

As search engines increasingly rely on AI technologies like NLP, machine learning, and AI content detection, SEO strategies must evolve to align with these advancements. It's important to create content that matches user intent, promotes engagement, and prioritizes human-centric value. By focusing on content that resonates with both users and AI-driven algorithms, SEO practitioners can improve visibility, build authority, and create a more meaningful search experience.

B. Voice and Visual Search Innovations

The rise of voice and visual search technologies represents a significant shift in the way users interact with search engines. These new search modalities have been fueled by advancements in AI and machine learning, enabling users to conduct searches using spoken commands or images instead of typed text. As voice assistants and visual recognition tools become more sophisticated, optimizing for these search methods offers businesses unique opportunities to connect with audiences in engaging ways. Let's explore how to optimize for voice and visual search to capture traffic from these emerging search channels.

1. Voice Search Optimization: Capturing Conversational Queries

Voice search has grown rapidly with the popularity of virtual assistants like Google Assistant, Alexa, and Siri. Unlike traditional text searches, voice searches are typically conversational, longer, and often phrased as questions. Voice search is especially important for local queries, where users seek quick, on-the-go answers. Optimizing for voice search involves understanding natural language patterns and focusing on content that delivers concise, direct answers.

- **How Voice Search Works**: Voice search technology uses NLP to interpret spoken language, understanding user intent based on phrasing, tone, and context. Voice search queries are usually more specific and intent-driven, often including words like "how," "what," "best," or "near me." For example, a user might ask, "Where can I find the best pizza near me?" or "How do I make gluten-free pasta?" Voice search algorithms then prioritize results that can provide quick, accurate answers.

- **How to Optimize for Voice Search**:
  - **Use Conversational Language**: Write content that mimics natural speech patterns, addressing questions directly and using simple language. FAQs, for instance, can be an effective way to capture voice search traffic, as they answer common questions in a concise, straightforward format.
  - **Focus on Long-Tail Keywords and Questions**: Voice searches are often longer than text-based queries, so targeting long-tail keywords and question-based phrases is essential. Instead of just "gluten-free pasta," optimize for phrases like "how to make gluten-free pasta at home."
  - **Implement Structured Data**: Structured data, like schema markup, helps search engines understand the context and intent of your content, increasing its chances of appearing as a featured snippet or in voice search responses. For local businesses, adding schema for local SEO can improve the visibility of location-based voice searches.

- **Optimize for Featured Snippets**: Many voice search results pull directly from featured snippets, so crafting content that is snippet-friendly (using bullet points, numbered lists, or short answers) can improve your chances of appearing in voice search results.

2. Visual Search Optimization: Engaging Users Through Images and Visual Recognition

Visual search allows users to search using images instead of text, with tools like Google Lens, Pinterest Lens, and Bing Visual Search leading the way in visual recognition. Visual search is particularly useful in industries where products are highly visual, such as fashion, home decor, travel, and food. Optimizing for visual search enables businesses to capture users who prefer interacting with images or need specific information about objects they see in the real world.

- **How Visual Search Works**: Visual search technology uses machine learning to analyze an image and identify its contents, such as products, landmarks, or even text within an image. For example, a user can take a photo of a piece of furniture they like, and visual search will suggest similar products or link to relevant online stores. Visual search algorithms prioritize high-quality, informative images and rely on metadata to interpret the content accurately.
- **How to Optimize for Visual Search**:
  - **Use High-Quality Images**: Since visual search relies on image recognition, ensure your images are clear, high-resolution, and well-lit. Quality images help search engines correctly identify objects, increasing the likelihood of

appearing in visual search results.
- **Optimize Image Alt Text and File Names**: Add descriptive, keyword-rich alt text to each image, as this helps search engines understand the content of the image. Instead of "IMG1234.jpg," name the file descriptively, such as "modern-grey-leather-sofa.jpg."
- **Leverage Structured Data for Images**: Using schema markup for images, such as product schema or recipe schema, provides additional context to search engines. Structured data can increase the visibility of images in search results and improve relevance for visual search queries.
- **Create Pinterest-Optimized Content**: Pinterest is a popular platform for visual search, so creating visually appealing, shareable images on Pinterest can drive additional visual search traffic. Use vertical images with optimized descriptions and relevant hashtags to increase visibility on the platform.
- **Encourage User-Generated Content**: User-generated images, such as reviews with customer photos, can increase the number of visuals associated with your brand and improve the diversity of content available for visual searches.

Bringing It All Together: Optimizing for a Multimodal Search Experience

Voice and visual search innovations are changing the way users interact with search engines, making it essential for SEO practitioners to adapt their strategies. By optimizing for voice search, businesses can capture traffic from conversational, intent-driven queries, particularly for local and informational searches. Optimizing for visual search, meanwhile, is a powerful strategy for product-focused industries, where high-quality images and metadata help connect users with visually relevant content.

Together, voice and visual search represent a multimodal search landscape that broadens the ways users find information online. As these technologies continue to evolve, businesses that invest in voice and visual search optimization will be better positioned to reach audiences across different search channels, driving engagement and improving visibility in a rapidly changing SEO environment.

C. AI and Personalization

AI-driven personalization is reshaping search by delivering customized results and recommendations tailored to each user's preferences, behavior, and history. Rather than providing a one-size-fits-all list of results, search engines now use AI to create a more individualized experience that anticipates what users are most likely to find relevant and useful. Personalization in search impacts everything from the type of content displayed to the order of results, offering SEO practitioners new opportunities—and challenges—in optimizing for personalized experiences.

1. Customized Search Results: Tailoring Content to User Preferences

AI-powered algorithms use a combination of factors, such as search history, location, device, and past interactions, to customize search results. This means that two users entering the same query may see different results based on their unique profiles. By understanding what users have previously searched for, engaged with, or clicked on, AI enables search engines to deliver more relevant and engaging content that aligns with individual interests and needs.

- **How Customized Results Work**: AI uses machine learning to track and analyze patterns in user behavior. For example, if a user frequently searches for vegan recipes, their future searches about "healthy recipes" are more likely to show results that highlight vegan options. Google's personalized algorithms also take location into account, which is particularly beneficial for local queries; a search for "bookstores" will show results for bookstores near the user's current location.

- **Impact on SEO**: Customized results mean that SEO strategies must go beyond general optimization to consider specific user segments. For example, creating diverse content tailored to various user interests within your audience can increase the likelihood of capturing a wider range of personalized search results. Additionally, optimizing for local SEO, mobile experience, and other user-specific factors can help ensure that content resonates with personalized preferences, increasing engagement and relevance for individual users.

- **How to Optimize for Customized Results**:
  - **Segment Content for Different Audiences**: Identify key audience segments within your target demographic and create content that appeals to their unique needs. For instance, a fitness site might produce content tailored to beginners, advanced athletes, and those with specific health concerns.
  - **Leverage Location-Based Keywords**: Include local keywords where relevant to capture users in specific geographic areas. Even if your business isn't exclusively local, adding location-specific information can increase visibility for

users in that area.
- **Encourage User Engagement**: The more users engage with your site, the more likely it is that your content will appear in their personalized search results. Encourage repeat visits through valuable content, email newsletters, and social media engagement to build a loyal audience that returns to your site.

2. Personalized Recommendations: Enhancing Engagement and Discoverability

Personalized recommendations are a powerful tool for keeping users engaged with relevant content based on their past interactions. AI-driven recommendation engines analyze user behavior to suggest similar or complementary content, products, or services that match their interests. These recommendations are often seen on e-commerce platforms, content-heavy sites, and streaming services, where they improve discoverability and keep users engaged.

- **How Personalized Recommendations Work**: Recommendation engines use collaborative filtering, content-based filtering, or a hybrid of both to analyze data and make suggestions. Collaborative filtering analyzes user behavior patterns across groups of users, while content-based filtering focuses on the characteristics of the content itself. For example, if a user frequently reads articles about eco-friendly products, the recommendation engine might suggest related content or products, increasing the likelihood of further engagement.
- **Impact on SEO and Content Strategy**: Personalized recommendations help extend user sessions, which can improve SEO metrics like dwell

time and reduce bounce rates—factors that search engines interpret as indicators of quality content. For SEO, this means creating interconnected content that encourages users to explore more. E-commerce sites, in particular, benefit from personalized product suggestions, which can drive conversions and increase the site's overall relevance for similar search queries.

- **How to Optimize for Personalized Recommendations**:
    - **Implement Related Content Links**: On blog posts and articles, add links to related content, such as "You might also like" or "Related articles." This encourages users to explore additional pages, increasing engagement and session duration.
    - **Use Product or Content Tagging**: For e-commerce or content-heavy sites, tag products or articles by categories and attributes (e.g., "eco-friendly," "best-seller," "new arrivals") to improve recommendation accuracy.
    - **Leverage Internal Linking**: Use strategic internal linking to connect pages across similar themes or user interests. This helps search engines understand the relationships between content pieces and makes it easier for users to discover relevant pages.

Bringing It All Together: Optimizing for Personalized Search

AI and personalization are transforming search from a standardized experience to one that is highly tailored to individual users. For SEO professionals, this shift underscores the importance of creating diverse, engaging, and relevant content that aligns with varied user preferences. By focusing on customized results and personalized recommendations, businesses can build deeper connections with their audiences, fostering engagement and encouraging repeat visits.

Chapter 6. Optimizing Websites for Traditional and AI-Powered SEO

As search engines evolve with AI-driven algorithms and user expectations become more sophisticated, the strategies for website optimization must adapt to meet both traditional and AI-powered SEO demands. Traditional SEO focuses on established practices like keyword targeting, site structure, and link building, while AI-powered SEO emphasizes contextual understanding, personalization, and user engagement. To succeed, websites must balance foundational SEO principles with cutting-edge techniques that cater to AI's growing role in search.

A. Advanced Keyword Research Strategies

Keyword research has evolved beyond simple keyword matching to encompass strategies that align with search engines' advanced understanding of language and context. With the rise of semantic search and the importance of topic clustering, effective keyword research now requires a more sophisticated approach that addresses user intent and relevance on a deeper level. By employing semantic search and topic clustering strategies, SEO professionals can create content that resonates with both traditional and AI-powered search engines, helping to improve visibility, engagement, and search rankings.

1. Semantic Search: Focusing on Meaning and Context

Semantic search is an AI-driven approach that enables search engines to interpret the intent and context behind user queries rather than simply matching individual keywords. This means that search engines look for the overall meaning of a query and prioritize content that answers the question holistically. Semantic search considers synonyms, related terms, and context to deliver more accurate results, making it essential for SEO practitioners to think beyond isolated keywords.

- **How Semantic Search Works**: Semantic search algorithms, like Google's Hummingbird, analyze the relationships between words and interpret user intent based on the query's context. For instance, if a user searches for "best places to eat in Chicago," the search engine considers terms related to dining, restaurants, and reviews instead of focusing only on "eat" and "Chicago." This ensures that users receive results that directly satisfy their intent, even if the exact keywords don't match.

- **How to Optimize for Semantic Search**:
    - **Use Natural Language and Related Keywords**: Include phrases and terms that naturally flow within the content and cover various aspects of the topic. Use tools like Google's "People Also Ask" and related searches to find associated phrases and questions that align with the primary keyword.
    - **Focus on Intent and Depth**: Develop content that fully addresses the user's query, covering multiple angles and providing valuable insights. For example, an article titled "The Complete Guide to Dining in Chicago" might discuss popular neighborhoods, dining styles, price ranges, and seasonal food events.
    - **Implement Structured Data**: Structured data, like schema markup, helps search engines understand the context of your content and associate it with related topics, which is especially useful for semantic search. Mark up

your content with relevant schema types (e.g., reviews, local business, recipes) to enhance search visibility.

2. Topic Clustering: Organizing Content Around Core Themes

Topic clustering is a content organization strategy that groups related pieces of content around a central theme, or "pillar." Each pillar page provides an overview of a broad topic and links to in-depth articles on subtopics, creating a structured network of interlinked content. Topic clusters improve SEO by signaling to search engines that your site covers a subject comprehensively, enhancing authority and relevance for broad search queries.

- **How Topic Clustering Works**: In a topic cluster, a pillar page serves as the main hub for a core topic, such as "Digital Marketing." Linked to this pillar are cluster pages that dive deeper into specific subtopics, like "Social Media Marketing," "Content Marketing Strategy," and "Email Marketing Best Practices." This structure helps search engines understand the relationships between your content, improving visibility for both the pillar and cluster pages.

- **How to Optimize for Topic Clustering**:
  - **Identify Core Topics and Subtopics**: Use keyword research and audience insights to identify high-level topics that align with your audience's interests and frequently searched terms. For example, if "Digital Marketing" is your core topic, consider subtopics like "SEO Basics," "PPC Advertising," and "Video Marketing Tips."
  - **Create Comprehensive Pillar Pages**: Pillar pages should cover a broad topic in depth

but leave room for further exploration through internal links to related cluster pages. For instance, a pillar page on "Digital Marketing" could provide a high-level overview with links to more detailed articles on SEO, social media, and content strategy.
  - **Link Strategically Between Pillar and Cluster Pages**: Internal links between the pillar and cluster pages help users navigate your content and signal to search engines that these pages are part of a cohesive content structure. This internal linking strategy strengthens the authority of your pillar page while enhancing the relevance of individual cluster pages.

Bringing It All Together: A Unified Approach to Advanced Keyword Research

By combining semantic search and topic clustering, SEO professionals can develop a keyword strategy that aligns with modern search engine algorithms and meets user expectations for comprehensive, context-rich content. Semantic search encourages a focus on meaning and intent, while topic clustering structures content to showcase expertise and depth. Together, these strategies create a unified approach to keyword research that prioritizes both relevance and authority, making it easier for search engines to understand and rank your content effectively.

B. Crafting High-Quality, AI-Friendly Content

Creating content that appeals to both human readers and AI-driven algorithms is essential. With search engines becoming more sophisticated in understanding context, intent, and quality, the key to success lies in balancing user-centric content with SEO principles. Writing for humans and algorithms involves crafting informative, engaging, and well-structured content that resonates with audiences while also meeting the technical requirements of AI-driven search engines. Let's explore strategies for creating high-quality, AI-friendly content that satisfies both search engines and users.

1. Writing for Humans: Prioritizing Value, Clarity, and Engagement

The core of effective content is creating genuine value for readers. When content addresses real needs, answers questions, and provides actionable insights, it naturally resonates with audiences. Writing for humans means focusing on clarity, readability, and relevance to ensure that users find your content informative and enjoyable.

- **How to Prioritize Value**: Ensure that each piece of content answers a specific question or fulfills a particular need. Conduct audience research to understand what users are searching for, then create content that addresses those topics thoroughly. For example, an article on "how to start a small business" should cover everything from initial planning to funding options and legal considerations.

- **Improving Readability**: Break content into short paragraphs, use headings and subheadings, and include bullet points or numbered lists where appropriate. Clear formatting makes content more accessible, allowing readers to find information quickly. Use simple, conversational language to make the content approachable, avoiding jargon unless absolutely necessary.

- **Enhancing Engagement**: Use storytelling elements, relatable examples, and interactive media (e.g., images, videos, infographics) to keep readers interested. Engaging content not only enhances the user experience but also increases metrics like time on page and click-through rate, which positively impact SEO.

2. Writing for Algorithms: Structuring Content for Search Engines

While content should prioritize the user experience, it's also essential to structure it in a way that helps search engines understand its context and relevance. Algorithms analyze specific elements of content, including keywords, headings, structure, and metadata, to determine its suitability for search results.

- **Keyword Optimization**: Use primary and related keywords naturally throughout the content, especially in headings, the introduction, and concluding sections. Avoid overstuffing keywords, which can detract from readability and may result in penalties. Instead, focus on contextual keyword usage, aligning with the natural flow of information.

- **Using Structured Data and Metadata**: Metadata, such as title tags and meta descriptions, help algorithms interpret content and improve click-through rates. Include keywords in metadata and ensure that each title and description is concise, informative, and reflective of the content. Additionally, apply structured data (schema markup) to enhance content appearance in search results, such as star ratings, FAQs, and review snippets.

- **Organizing with Headings and Lists**: Use clear headings (H1, H2, H3) to organize content logically, signaling to algorithms that the page covers multiple subtopics. Search engines prioritize well-structured content because it's easier to analyze and understand. Headings also improve user experience by breaking down information into scannable sections, allowing readers to locate key points quickly.

3. Combining Human-Centric and Algorithm-Friendly Practices

Creating AI-friendly content doesn't mean sacrificing user experience for algorithms. Instead, the best content combines high-quality writing for humans with technical structuring for search engines, providing a holistic approach to SEO.

- **Address User Intent**: Understand the intent behind each target keyword to create content that aligns with what users genuinely want to know. If a user searches for "benefits of yoga," for example, they are likely looking for specific advantages like stress reduction, flexibility improvement, and overall wellness. Content that matches this intent is more likely to rank and satisfy readers.

- **Optimize for Featured Snippets and Voice Search**: Structured content that answers questions concisely and clearly is more likely to appear as a featured snippet or be used in voice search results. Use question-based subheadings and provide brief, direct answers before diving into more detailed explanations. Lists, tables, and short paragraphs are particularly effective for capturing featured snippets

- **Leverage AI Content Detection and Avoid Over-Optimization**: As search engines increasingly use AI to detect and assess content quality, overly optimized or automated content can be flagged as low-value. Avoid practices like keyword stuffing, repetitive phrases, or generic AI-generated text. If AI is used in content creation, refine the output to add depth, originality, and unique perspectives that reflect human input.

Bringing It All Together: Creating Content that Excels

Writing high-quality, AI-friendly content requires a balance between delivering value to users and meeting technical criteria for search engines. By focusing on content that is informative, well-structured, and contextually rich, SEO professionals can appeal to both audiences, enhancing engagement and visibility. As AI-driven algorithms continue to evolve, content that emphasizes user satisfaction while remaining accessible to search engines will be key to SEO success.

C. Enhancing Technical SEO

Technical SEO is the backbone of a website's ability to be crawled, indexed, and understood by search engines. Structured data, schema markup, and the implementation of JSON-LD are essential elements in creating a clear, organized structure that enhances search engines' understanding of your content. These tools not only improve how search engines interpret your site's information but also increase the likelihood of your content appearing in rich results, such as featured snippets, knowledge panels, and other visually enhanced formats. Let's explore these technical SEO practices and how they can help boost your site's visibility and user engagement.

1. Structured Data and Schema Markup: Providing

Context to Search Engines

Structured data is a standardized format for providing information about a page and classifying its content. Schema markup is a type of structured data that helps search engines understand specific elements on a page, such as products, reviews, recipes, events, and more. By using schema, SEO professionals can provide additional context to search engines, improving the site's relevance and appearance in search results.

- **How Structured Data and Schema Markup Work**: Schema markup tags information in a way that helps search engines categorize content more accurately. For instance, a recipe page with schema markup will include structured data that identifies the recipe's name, ingredients, cook time, and calories, allowing search engines to showcase this information in a clear, user-friendly format. Schema helps search engines connect the content to specific queries, making it easier for users to find exactly what they're looking for.

- **Benefits of Schema Markup for SEO**: Schema can improve click-through rates (CTR) by displaying rich snippets that draw attention, such as ratings, images, and pricing. These enhanced results can make listings more attractive to users, which can increase traffic and engagement. Schema also increases the likelihood of appearing in knowledge panels and other SERP features, which can improve brand visibility and authority.

- **How to Implement Schema Markup**: Identify the most relevant schema types for your content. Common types include "Product," "Recipe," "Event," "Article," and "Local Business." Use Google's Structured Data Markup Helper or schema.org to find the appropriate tags, and apply them to your HTML code to ensure accurate classification. For instance, an online store might use "Product" schema to highlight item prices, availability, and ratings directly in search results.

2. Implementing JSON-LD for Rich Results: Simplifying Structured Data

JSON-LD (JavaScript Object Notation for Linked Data) is the recommended format for adding structured data to your website. JSON-LD is widely preferred over other formats like Microdata and RDFa because it's easier to implement, doesn't interfere with the HTML structure, and is compatible with most search engines. JSON-LD is particularly effective for creating rich results, as it makes it easier for search engines to process and understand content.

- **How JSON-LD Works**: JSON-LD allows you to add structured data as a JavaScript object within your HTML code. Unlike in-line markup, JSON-LD data can be placed within the <head> or <body> of the page without altering the visible content or layout. For example, JSON-LD can be used to tag key details for a product page, like the product name, description, price, and availability, which then appear as enhanced elements in search results.

- **Advantages of JSON-LD for SEO**: JSON-LD is more adaptable and doesn't require embedding tags throughout HTML, making it a simpler and cleaner option for structured data. This format is also favored by Google, making it more likely to be processed accurately. Implementing JSON-LD increases the chances of earning rich results, like carousels, reviews, and FAQ snippets, which enhance visibility and attract user attention.

- **How to Implement JSON-LD: Use Schema Generators**: Tools like Google's Structured Data Markup Helper, Schema Markup Generator, or JSON-LD Playground can help you create JSON-LD code for your content type.
    - **Add the JSON-LD Code to Your HTML**: Insert the generated JSON-LD code into the <head> or <body> section of your webpage. For example, if you're implementing JSON-LD for an FAQ page, your code will define each question and answer so that search engines can recognize the structure.
    - **Test and Validate**: Use Google's Rich Results Test and Schema Markup Validator to verify that your JSON-LD code is correctly implemented and meets Google's guidelines. This step ensures that your structured data is properly formatted and can produce the desired rich results.

Bringing It All Together: The Role of Structured Data and JSON-LD in SEO

Enhancing technical SEO with structured data, schema markup, and JSON-LD implementation is essential for improving how search engines understand and display your content. By using schema to provide context and implementing JSON-LD to simplify structured data, you can significantly boost your chances of appearing in rich results. These optimizations make your listings more engaging and accessible, increasing visibility, CTR, and overall user satisfaction.

D. Improving User Experience (UX)

A positive user experience (UX) is essential for both SEO and overall site success. When users find a site easy to navigate, readable, and accessible, they're more likely to engage, return, and share it—signals that search engines interpret as indicators of high-quality content. By enhancing site navigation, readability, and accessibility, you can create a seamless experience that meets diverse user needs and aligns with SEO objectives. Let's explore these UX elements and strategies for optimizing them.

1. Site Navigation: Ensuring Intuitive and Efficient User Flow

Effective site navigation is the foundation of a good user experience. When users can easily locate what they're looking for, they're more likely to stay on the site, engage with the content, and complete actions. A well-organized navigation structure not only improves user experience but also helps search engines crawl and index pages more efficiently.

- **How to Optimize Site Navigation**:
    - **Use a Clear Menu Structure**: Organize your primary navigation menu with clear, descriptive labels for each section. Categories and subcategories should be logical and intuitive, helping users locate information with minimal effort. For example, an e-commerce site could use categories like "Men," "Women," and "Kids" in the main menu, with subcategories for specific types of products.
    - **Include Breadcrumbs**: Breadcrumb navigation helps users understand their location within the site hierarchy and easily backtrack. This feature enhances usability, especially on larger sites, by providing a clear path to navigate between categories and subcategories.
    - **Simplify the User Journey**: Avoid overwhelming users with too many menu

options or layers of navigation. Prioritize high-value pages and use dropdown menus judiciously to prevent clutter. Include a prominent search bar so users can quickly find specific content if it's not immediately visible in the main menu.

2. Readability: Crafting Content That's Easy to Digest

Readability is a critical aspect of UX, ensuring that users can quickly absorb information without struggling with dense or complicated text. Well-organized, readable content increases user engagement, reduces bounce rates, and can improve SEO performance by keeping users on the page longer.

- **How to Improve Readability**:
    - **Use Clear and Simple Language**: Write in a conversational tone and avoid jargon or overly complex sentences unless they're necessary for the content's context. Aim to keep sentences concise and paragraphs short to make content more approachable.
    - **Structure Content with Headings and Subheadings**: Break down content into sections using H2 and H3 headings, which guide users through the information and make it easier to scan. Well-organized headings not only improve readability but also signal content structure to search engines.
    - **Optimize Font and Spacing**: Use fonts that are easy to read across devices, and ensure a comfortable font size, typically around 16px for body text. Use sufficient line spacing and white space to prevent text from appearing crowded. Good spacing helps reduce visual fatigue, especially for mobile users.

3. Accessibility: Making Your Site Usable for All Audiences

Accessibility ensures that users of all abilities can navigate and interact with your site. An accessible site is designed with inclusivity in mind, allowing people with disabilities, such as visual or motor impairments, to access and enjoy your content. Search engines also prioritize accessibility as part of user-centric design, which aligns with SEO objectives.

- **How to Improve Accessibility**:
    - **Use Descriptive Alt Text for Images**: Alt text helps screen readers interpret images for visually impaired users. It also provides context to search engines, enhancing the chances of appearing in image search results. Make alt text specific and descriptive, explaining the content and purpose of the image.
    - **Provide Keyboard Navigation Options**: Ensure that users can navigate your site using keyboard shortcuts alone. This includes enabling keyboard focus on menus, forms, and interactive elements, which benefits users with motor disabilities who may not use a mouse.
    - **Implement ARIA (Accessible Rich Internet Applications) Roles and Labels**: ARIA attributes improve accessibility for users with screen readers by defining elements on a webpage. For example, ARIA roles can specify the function of buttons, forms, and other interactive elements, making it easier for assistive technologies to interpret the content.

Bringing It All Together: Creating a User-Centric Experience

Improving UX through optimized navigation, readability, and accessibility is key to engaging and retaining users while meeting SEO goals. A user-friendly site encourages positive engagement metrics, such as increased time on page and reduced bounce rates, which signal quality to search engines. By creating a seamless, accessible experience, you're building a foundation that benefits both users and search engine performance.

E. Leveraging Multimedia Content

Multimedia content—including images, videos, and podcasts—plays a powerful role in creating a dynamic, engaging user experience. When optimized effectively, multimedia can enhance SEO by improving engagement metrics, increasing visibility in multimedia search results, and appealing to users with different content preferences. Multimedia content also has a unique advantage in capturing users' attention, encouraging them to spend more time on your site and explore further. Let's explore strategies for optimizing images, videos, and podcasts to maximize their SEO and user experience benefits.

1. Optimizing Images: Enhancing Visual Appeal and Accessibility

Images are essential for creating a visually engaging experience, especially on product pages, blogs, and other content-rich sections of a site. However, without proper optimization, images can slow down page load times and negatively impact user experience. Optimizing images ensures they load quickly and provide value for both users and search engines.

- **How to Optimize Images:**
    - **Use Descriptive, Keyword-Rich Alt Text**: Alt text provides context for images, especially for visually impaired users relying on screen readers. Include descriptive, concise, and keyword-rich alt text to help search engines understand the content of the image, which can improve image search rankings. For instance, instead of "IMG123.jpg," an optimized alt text for a product image might be "black leather handbag with gold accents."
    - **Compress Image Files for Faster Loading**: Large image files can significantly slow down page load times. Use image compression tools like TinyPNG or JPEG-Optimizer to reduce file size without compromising quality. Opt for modern image formats like WebP, which provide high-quality visuals with smaller file sizes.
    - **Implement Structured Data for Images**: Using schema markup for images can increase the chances of appearing in rich results. For example, adding structured data to product images can display pricing, availability, and reviews directly in search results, making your content more visually appealing to users.

2. Optimizing Videos: Driving Engagement and Enhancing SEO Visibility

Videos are among the most engaging forms of multimedia content, with the ability to boost dwell time, attract backlinks, and even appear in dedicated video search results. Video content is particularly effective for tutorials, product demonstrations, customer testimonials, and storytelling, allowing businesses to deliver complex information in an easily digestible format.

- **How to Optimize Videos**:
  - **Add Descriptive Titles, Descriptions, and Tags**: Video titles, descriptions, and tags help search engines understand the content of your video. Include relevant keywords in the title and description to improve search visibility. For example, a title like "How to Make a Perfect Cup of Coffee" is more descriptive than "Coffee Tutorial."
  - **Use Video Schema Markup**: Adding structured data to your videos, such as VideoObject schema, can increase the likelihood of appearing in video-rich snippets. This markup allows you to specify details like video duration, upload date, and thumbnail, making your video more accessible to search engines and more appealing in SERPs.
  - **Host Videos on Platforms that Support SEO Goals**: While embedding videos from platforms like YouTube can drive traffic, consider hosting high-priority videos directly on your site to improve on-site engagement. Videos hosted on YouTube may drive more off-site traffic, so balance video placement based on your goals.
  - **Add Transcripts for Accessibility and SEO**: Providing transcripts for videos benefits accessibility, as it allows users with hearing impairments to engage with your content. Transcripts also create additional text for search engines to crawl, which can improve keyword relevance and search visibility.

3. Optimizing Podcasts: Increasing Discoverability and Engagement

Podcasts are rapidly gaining popularity and are an excellent way to engage users through in-depth discussions, interviews, and storytelling. With proper optimization, podcasts can drive engagement and traffic, especially if they're available in both audio and text formats.

- **How to Optimize Podcasts**:
  - **Add Descriptive Titles, Descriptions, and Episode Summaries**: Similar to video optimization, include keywords in your podcast titles and descriptions to enhance discoverability. An episode title like "Expert Tips for Growing Your Small Business" is more informative than simply "Episode 5."
  - **Provide Full Transcripts or Show Notes**: Podcast transcripts or show notes improve accessibility and provide search engines with text to crawl. Transcripts make it easier for users to search for specific topics discussed in the episode and increase the podcast's overall visibility.
  - **Leverage Podcast Schema Markup**: Use structured data (such as Podcast schema) to enhance the visibility of your podcast episodes in search results. Schema markup can include details like episode number, guest names, and topics covered, helping search engines interpret and display your podcast content more effectively.
  - **Submit Your Podcast to Popular Platforms**: Make your podcast available on platforms like Spotify, Apple Podcasts, and Google Podcasts, which can help reach new audiences. Include links to your podcast from your site and encourage users to engage by subscribing, leaving reviews, or sharing episodes on social media.

Bringing It All Together: Integrating Multimedia for a Comprehensive SEO Strategy

Leveraging multimedia content—including optimized images, videos, and podcasts—not only enhances user experience but also provides valuable SEO benefits by diversifying content offerings and improving engagement. By optimizing each type of multimedia with descriptive text, schema markup, and proper formatting, you increase your chances of appearing in multimedia search results and creating a memorable, dynamic experience for users.

Chapter 7. Optimizing for AI Search Platforms and Assistants

As AI-driven search platforms and virtual assistants become more integrated into everyday life, optimizing for these technologies presents new opportunities and challenges for businesses. Unlike traditional search engines, AI platforms like Siri, Alexa, and Google Assistant rely on natural language processing and machine learning to interpret conversational queries and provide immediate answers. Optimizing for AI search requires a focus on voice search, featured snippets, and structured data, allowing businesses to capture user attention through these highly interactive and personalized channels.

A. Overview of AI Search Platforms

AI search platforms have transformed the way users interact with information by providing fast, accurate, and often conversational responses to queries. Platforms like *Google Assistant*, *ChatGPT*, *Perplexity*, *Siri*, *Alexa*, and *Cortana* each offer unique functionalities and operate on advanced algorithms designed to interpret natural language, contextualize queries, and deliver precise answers. Understanding the differences and capabilities of these platforms is essential for optimizing content that resonates across various AI-driven environments.

1. Google Assistant: Leading in Conversational Search

Google Assistant is a versatile, AI-powered virtual assistant integrated into Android devices, Google Home, and other Google services. Leveraging Google's extensive search engine database, Assistant provides direct answers to queries, making it a go-to for voice search optimization.

- **Key Features**: Google Assistant supports a wide range of tasks, from answering questions to controlling smart home devices. It prioritizes content that ranks well on Google's search engine, particularly content that appears in featured snippets.

- **Optimization Tips**: Focus on creating concise, direct answers to common questions that are likely to be used as featured snippets. Structured data, especially FAQ and How-To schema, enhances the visibility of content optimized for Google Assistant.

2. ChatGPT: Conversational AI for In-Depth Responses

OpenAI's ChatGPT is designed to facilitate detailed, conversational interactions and can provide in-depth responses on a variety of topics. While not a traditional search engine, ChatGPT's AI-driven response generation allows users to ask complex questions and receive comprehensive answers, making it valuable for deeper information searches.

- **Key Features**: ChatGPT excels at contextualizing longer conversations, providing answers, explanations, and solutions in natural, human-like language.

- **Optimization Tips**: Focus on creating well-structured, informative content that covers topics in depth. Content that is fact-based, detailed, and comprehensive performs best, as ChatGPT draws on a broad range of pre-existing text data to generate responses.

3. Perplexity: AI-Enhanced Knowledge Retrieval

Perplexity AI combines elements of search and AI to provide succinct, informative responses by aggregating knowledge from multiple sources. It is particularly effective for factual information, offering quick insights and citations from reliable sources.

- **Key Features**: Perplexity AI provides concise responses with source attribution, making it ideal for users looking for brief but accurate answers.
- **Optimization Tips**: Provide fact-based, well-sourced content that can be quickly referenced. Using citations and structuring information in concise segments can increase the likelihood of your content being referenced by Perplexity.

4. Siri: Apple's Voice-Activated Search Assistant

Siri, Apple's virtual assistant, is built into iOS devices and offers a voice-activated, conversational search experience. Siri focuses on local search, simple queries, and tasks like setting reminders or sending messages, often leveraging Apple's own data sources, as well as Bing for web searches.

- **Key Features**: Siri emphasizes local search and integrates with apps and functions within the Apple ecosystem, making it particularly useful for location-based and device-specific queries.
- **Optimization Tips**: Optimize for local SEO to capture Siri-based queries, especially for location-based searches. Using structured data for local businesses, such as location schema, enhances visibility on Siri.

5. Alexa: Amazon's Assistant for Voice-Activated Commerce and Information

Amazon's Alexa, integrated into Echo devices, offers a robust voice search experience with a focus on smart home control, shopping, and general knowledge queries. Alexa can answer factual questions, play music, and facilitate online purchases, making it central to e-commerce SEO.

- **Key Features**: Alexa emphasizes e-commerce functionality, smart home integration, and localized content.
- **Optimization Tips**: For product-related searches, ensure product listings are optimized with clear descriptions, accurate prices, and customer reviews. Structured data, particularly product schema, improves the chance of visibility on Alexa-driven searches.

6. Cortana: Microsoft's Digital Assistant for Productivity

Cortana, Microsoft's virtual assistant, is designed for productivity-related tasks, providing reminders, calendar management, and integration with Microsoft products. Although less focused on general web search, Cortana integrates with Bing for external information.

- **Key Features**: Cortana specializes in productivity and device integration within the Microsoft ecosystem, using Bing as its primary search engine.
- **Optimization Tips**: Focus on optimizing for Bing with concise, factual content, particularly for information that aligns with productivity and work-related queries. Business listings optimized for Bing can improve local search visibility on Cortana.

Bringing It All Together: Tailoring Content for AI Search Platforms

Each AI search platform has its unique characteristics and priorities, from Google Assistant's preference for snippet-optimized answers to ChatGPT's conversational approach. By understanding and aligning content with the specific strengths of each platform, SEO professionals can create a more targeted and effective strategy that ensures visibility and relevance across AI-driven search environments. In the next sections, we'll delve into actionable strategies to optimize content for these platforms, ensuring a comprehensive approach to AI-focused SEO.

B. How AI Assistants Source and Present Information

AI assistants rely on a variety of sources to deliver concise, accurate, and relevant responses to user queries. By drawing information from featured snippets, knowledge graphs, and review platforms like Yelp, AI search platforms and assistants are able to provide users with high-quality, context-rich answers that often appear instantaneously. Each of these information sources has its unique structure, function, and influence on search visibility, making it essential for SEO practitioners to understand how to optimize content for these formats. Let's explore how featured snippets, knowledge graphs, and review platforms power AI assistants and the strategies for optimizing content for these sources.

1. Featured Snippets: Providing Direct Answers to Queries

Featured snippets are short, highlighted sections that appear at the top of Google's search results, delivering quick answers to common questions. These snippets are especially important for AI assistants like Google Assistant and Siri, which often pull responses directly from them. Featured snippets come in various formats—paragraphs, lists, tables, and videos—and are designed to provide users with immediate answers without requiring them to click through to a webpage.

- **How Featured Snippets Work**: Featured snippets are selected from web content based on relevance, clarity, and conciseness. Google's algorithms prioritize pages that provide direct answers to specific questions, with snippets often appearing for "how-to," "what is," and "why" queries. When users ask a question to an AI assistant, it frequently pulls the snippet content to provide a quick, conversational answer.

- **How to Optimize for Featured Snippets**:
    - **Use Question-Based Headings**: Frame your headings in the form of questions that users commonly search for, like "What are the benefits of meditation?" or "How to optimize for featured snippets?".
    - **Provide Concise, Direct Answers**: In the first paragraph following the question, give a clear, direct answer, ideally in one to two sentences. You can then expand on the topic in subsequent paragraphs.
    - **Format for Different Snippet Types**: Use bullet points, numbered lists, or tables where applicable, as these formats are often featured for "how-to" and comparison queries. Structuring your content to match these snippet formats increases the chances of being selected.

2. Knowledge Graphs: Enriching Search Results with Structured Information

The Knowledge Graph is Google's semantic search feature that gathers data from multiple sources to provide comprehensive, fact-based information about people, places, organizations, and other entities. Knowledge graphs are presented in a separate panel on the search results page, giving users a rich overview of a topic without needing to click through. AI assistants use knowledge graphs to answer factual and broad-topic questions with reliable, authoritative data.

- **How Knowledge Graphs Work**: Knowledge graphs pull information from structured sources such as Wikipedia, government databases, and authoritative websites, creating a network of interrelated facts. The data is presented in a visually organized panel, showing key details, related entities, and often images. When a user asks an AI assistant for information about a well-known topic, the assistant may source data from the knowledge graph.

- **How to Optimize for Knowledge Graph Inclusion**:
    - **Ensure Accurate Information on Authoritative Sites**: Knowledge graphs rely heavily on data from recognized sites like Wikipedia, so contributing to these platforms with accurate, verified information about your brand, product, or service can improve chances of inclusion.
    - **Use Schema Markup**: Adding schema markup to your website's content, such as organization, person, and event schema, increases the likelihood of being included in the knowledge graph. Schema markup allows search engines to better understand and link your content to broader knowledge graphs.

- **Build Authority with Reliable Sources**: Secure mentions and citations on reputable sites, as knowledge graphs pull information from sources deemed highly authoritative. For example, creating consistent listings across industry directories and news platforms can enhance your brand's visibility in the knowledge graph.

3. Review Platforms: Influencing Local and Product-Based Searches

Review platforms like Yelp, TripAdvisor, and Google My Business play a crucial role in AI assistants' responses for location-based and product-specific queries. User-generated reviews, ratings, and business information on these platforms help AI assistants provide more nuanced, trust-based responses, especially for queries that involve recommendations, services, or experiences.

- **How Review Platforms Work**: Review platforms aggregate user feedback, ratings, and business details to provide potential customers with insights into the quality and reputation of a business. AI assistants rely on this data for questions like "Where's the best pizza place near me?" or "Find a top-rated plumber in my area." Review platforms also provide structured data that AI assistants can use for accurate and relevant responses.

- **How to Optimize for Review Platforms**:
  - **Claim and Optimize Business Listings**: Ensure your business is claimed on major review platforms like Google My Business, Yelp, and industry-specific directories. Complete each profile with accurate information, hours, contact details, and images to improve visibility.

- **Encourage Positive Reviews**: High ratings and positive feedback can improve your business's chances of appearing in AI assistant responses for local search queries. Encourage satisfied customers to leave reviews, and respond to both positive and negative feedback to demonstrate customer service and engagement.
- **Use Structured Data for Reviews**: Implement review schema markup on your website to display customer ratings and testimonials directly on your product or service pages. This can help search engines display review-based information more prominently and may increase click-through rates from users.

Bringing It All Together: Optimizing for AI Assistant Information Sources

AI assistants rely on featured snippets, knowledge graphs, and review platforms to deliver fast, relevant, and trustworthy answers to users. By understanding how each source functions and tailoring content to meet these criteria, businesses can improve their chances of being featured by AI assistants and reaching a broader audience.

C. Strategies for Gaining Visibility on AI Platforms

To ensure that your business is effectively represented across AI search platforms, it's essential to tailor content to meet the specific needs of these emerging technologies. AI platforms respond to conversational queries, prioritize fast answers, and often pull data from structured sources. By focusing on creating natural, accessible content and designing your site to align with AI retrieval methods, you can increase visibility across platforms. Here are some effective strategies for optimizing content on AI-driven search platforms, including techniques in conversational formatting, FAQs, and Voice SEO.

1. Conversational Content: Engaging AI Users with Natural Language

AI-powered search platforms, including voice assistants, favor content that mirrors natural language. Unlike traditional typed queries, users often phrase questions conversationally, making it essential to produce content that reflects these language patterns. AI platforms also look for content that directly answers user inquiries, ensuring that responses are both helpful and easily understood.

- **How to Develop Conversational Content**:
    - **Adopt a Casual, Accessible Tone**: Write content that feels like a direct conversation with the user. Opt for clear, straightforward language, and avoid overly technical terms when possible.
    - **Address Questions Clearly and Directly**: Begin responses with a concise answer before providing additional context. For example, start with a straightforward solution, like "Turn off the main water supply to start fixing a leaky faucet," before expanding on detailed steps.
    - **Keep Sentences Short and Impactful**: Short sentences and simple language improve readability and make content more adaptable for AI-driven responses.

2. FAQ Sections: Organizing Content for Quick, Relevant Answers

Organizing content in an FAQ format can help AI platforms deliver fast, accurate answers to specific questions. FAQs are naturally structured to provide direct responses, making them highly useful for AI platforms that prioritize clarity and brevity. Well-crafted FAQs also increase the chances of appearing in rich search results, which can improve visibility.

- **How to Structure Effective FAQs**:
    - **Identify Common Queries**: Use keyword research tools to find questions your audience is frequently asking. AI platforms often pull information from structured questions that align with high-volume search phrases.
    - **Format Answers for Quick Retrieval**: For each FAQ, start with a concise answer and then offer supporting details if necessary. This structure makes it easy for AI platforms to extract direct answers, increasing your content's relevance for quick search results.
    - **Leverage Schema Markup for Enhanced Visibility**: Adding FAQ schema markup helps search engines interpret your FAQ section, improving the likelihood of appearing in AI-generated answers.

3. Voice SEO: Enhancing Content for Voice-Activated Searches

Optimizing for voice search is crucial in reaching users who rely on voice-activated assistants like Google Assistant, Siri, and Alexa. Voice queries tend to be longer and phrased more conversationally than text searches, often involving specific, intent-driven questions or location-based requests. Focusing on Voice SEO can help ensure that your content is easily discoverable through voice-based queries.

- **How to Optimize Content for Voice Search**:
    - **Focus on Long-Tail, Conversational Keywords**: Voice searches are typically more specific, so consider targeting long-tail keywords that reflect user intent, like "Where can I find vegan-friendly cafes near me?" or "Best way to grow indoor herbs."
    - **Emphasize Local Optimization**: Many voice searches involve location-specific requests. Ensure your business is accurately represented on Google My Business and other directories, and integrate local keywords in relevant content to capture nearby searchers.
    - **Implement Structured Data for Quick, Accurate Responses**: Adding structured data, such as How-To or LocalBusiness schema, helps AI-driven platforms understand the context of your content, making it more likely to be selected for voice responses.

Bringing It All Together: Building an AI-Friendly Content Strategy

To gain visibility on AI-driven platforms, content should prioritize clarity, accessibility, and responsiveness to user intent. Structuring your website with conversational content, clear FAQs, and voice SEO ensures that AI assistants and search platforms can easily find and interpret your business information. By optimizing for these AI-specific needs, you create a user-centric experience that aligns with the latest advancements in search technology, improving your reach and engagement.

D. Adapting to Zero-Click Searches

With the rise of zero-click searches, more users are finding answers directly on the search results page without needing to click through to a website. Zero-click searches occur when search engines, using rich snippets, knowledge panels, or quick answer boxes, provide users with the information they're looking for immediately. While this trend reduces traffic to websites, it also presents an opportunity to increase brand exposure. By optimizing for zero-click searches, businesses can enhance visibility, build authority, and make their brand a go-to source for information—no clicks required.

1. Optimizing for Featured Snippets: Securing Prime Position in Search Results

Featured snippets, also known as "position zero," are concise responses to user queries that appear at the top of search results. These snippets are a primary source of zero-click information, capturing attention and positioning brands as reliable sources. Although featured snippets may reduce direct clicks to a website, they offer significant brand exposure and credibility.

- **How to Optimize for Featured Snippets**:
  - **Answer Questions Directly**: Craft content that provides concise answers to common questions. Begin each response with a straightforward answer, followed by any necessary detail or supporting information.
  - **Format for Snippet-Friendly Content**: Use headers, bullet points, and numbered lists for content that lends itself to quick answers, such as "how-to" guides or lists of benefits. Clear formatting makes it easier for search engines to extract and display your content in snippets.

- **Use Structured Data**: Structured data, such as FAQ or How-To schema, can increase the chances of your content being selected as a featured snippet by providing additional context for search engines.

2. Leveraging Knowledge Panels: Enhancing Brand Authority and Credibility

Knowledge panels are information boxes that appear on the right side of search results, often displaying key details about organizations, people, or brands. They pull information from reliable sources and are particularly effective for establishing authority and brand recognition in zero-click searches. Knowledge panels allow users to find critical brand information without navigating away from the search page.

- **How to Optimize for Knowledge Panels**:
    - **Ensure Accurate Information on Authoritative Sites**: Knowledge panels frequently pull data from trusted sources like Wikipedia, LinkedIn, and major directories. Having consistent, accurate information across these platforms increases the likelihood of appearing in a knowledge panel.
    - **Use Structured Data and Verify Listings**: Apply structured data on your site to help search engines interpret and display your business information accurately. Additionally, claim your Google Knowledge Panel if available to manage and verify brand details directly.
    - **Secure Mentions on Reputable Sites**: Information in knowledge panels often relies on data from credible external sites. Building relationships with industry sites or getting coverage on reputable platforms can improve

the quality of information associated with your brand.

3. Utilizing FAQ and How-To Schema: Providing Direct Answers in SERPs

FAQ and How-To schema allow content to be displayed in an expanded format directly within search results, making it ideal for zero-click searches. By marking up commonly asked questions and step-by-step guides, brands can showcase their expertise and capture attention without needing users to click through to the website. This approach works especially well for product support, tutorials, and customer service content.

- **How to Use FAQ and How-To Schema**:
    - **Identify User-Driven Questions**: Research common questions users have about your brand or industry, then create concise, well-structured answers. Place these questions and answers in a dedicated FAQ section or as individual headings throughout your content.
    - **Implement Schema Markup for Enhanced Display**: Use FAQ and How-To schema to structure your content for search engines. This markup allows Google to feature your answers directly in the SERPs, enhancing visibility and user engagement.
    - **Keep Content Updated and Relevant**: Regularly review and update your FAQ and How-To content to ensure it remains accurate and aligned with current user needs. Outdated information can reduce credibility and limit the effectiveness of zero-click optimization.

Bringing It All Together: Strategies for Zero-Click Optimization

Adapting to zero-click searches involves creating content that meets users' needs directly within search results. By optimizing for featured snippets, knowledge panels, and FAQ schema, businesses can maximize brand exposure, build authority, and engage users without requiring clicks. These tactics allow your brand to remain visible and relevant, leveraging the zero-click trend to reinforce brand recognition and demonstrate expertise.

Chapter 8. Enhancing Online Presence Beyond Your Website

Maintaining an effective online presence goes beyond optimizing your own website. As users explore multiple channels—social media, review platforms, industry directories, and third-party content sites—businesses have more opportunities to connect with audiences and reinforce brand visibility. By strategically cultivating a presence across various platforms, brands can extend their reach, build credibility, and create touchpoints that drive engagement even when users aren't on their website.

A. Social Media Optimization for AI

Social media platforms have become a crucial part of maintaining an online presence, especially as AI-driven algorithms increasingly shape content visibility. Algorithm changes now prioritize engagement metrics, user preferences, and real-time relevance, making it essential to tailor social media strategies to these shifting dynamics. Optimizing for AI-driven social media algorithms helps ensure that your content reaches your target audience, fosters engagement, and enhances your brand's visibility. Let's explore how to adapt to algorithm changes and leverage engagement metrics to optimize your social media presence.

1. Adapting to Algorithm Changes: Staying Relevant in Dynamic Feeds

Social media algorithms are constantly evolving to improve user experience by delivering personalized, relevant content. Platforms like Facebook, Instagram, Twitter, and

LinkedIn use AI to prioritize posts that are likely to resonate with users based on factors like past behavior, interests, and engagement history. Understanding these algorithms helps brands create content that is more likely to appear in users' feeds.

- **How to Adapt to Algorithm Changes**:
    - **Focus on Quality and Relevance**: Algorithms prioritize content that is both high-quality and relevant to user interests. Create visually engaging, informative, and timely content that directly addresses your audience's needs and preferences.
    - **Post Consistently and at Optimal Times**: Regular posting and timing content releases for peak engagement hours can help maintain visibility. Experiment with different posting schedules and monitor engagement metrics to determine when your audience is most active.
    - **Utilize New Features**: Social platforms often prioritize their latest features, such as Instagram Reels or LinkedIn Stories, to encourage user adoption. Leveraging these features can improve content reach and visibility as the platform promotes them more heavily in the feed.

2. Leveraging Engagement Metrics: Boosting Content Reach and Interaction

AI algorithms on social media platforms use engagement metrics—such as likes, shares, comments, and click-through rates—as indicators of content relevance and popularity. Content that receives high engagement is more likely to be promoted within the platform, reaching a broader audience and boosting brand visibility.

- **How to Use Engagement Metrics to Enhance Visibility**:
    - **Encourage Interaction with Calls-to-Action (CTAs)**: Use CTAs that prompt users to engage, such as "Share your thoughts," "Tag a friend," or "Click to learn more." Engagement boosts visibility, so fostering interaction is key to helping your content rank higher within AI-driven algorithms.
    - **Respond to Comments and Messages**: Interaction doesn't end once the content is posted. By responding to comments and engaging with your audience, you build a stronger connection and encourage more future engagement, which AI algorithms interpret as positive signals.
    - **Monitor and Optimize Based on Performance**: Regularly analyze engagement metrics to see what types of content resonate most with your audience. Use insights from high-performing posts to shape your content strategy, replicating elements that drive engagement.

3. Optimizing Content for AI-Powered Social Searches

With the integration of AI-powered search functions on social media platforms, users are able to find specific content based on keywords, topics, and hashtags more easily. Optimizing your posts for these search capabilities can increase discoverability and attract users searching for content in your industry or niche.

- **How to Optimize Content for Social Searches**:
    - **Use Relevant Hashtags**: Hashtags help categorize content and make it searchable within the platform. Research trending or high-

relevance hashtags within your industry to improve your content's discoverability in AI-powered searches.
- **Incorporate Keywords in Captions and Descriptions**: Just as with SEO, using relevant keywords in your social media captions, alt text for images, and video descriptions can improve your content's visibility in search results. Include keywords that match your target audience's interests.
- **Create Evergreen Content**: While trends change, evergreen content—such as how-to guides, tips, and educational content—remains relevant over time. AI algorithms may prioritize evergreen content that consistently attracts views and engagement, increasing long-term visibility.

Bringing It All Together: Building a Robust AI-Optimized Social Media Strategy

Optimizing for AI-driven social media algorithms requires a blend of strategic content creation, consistent engagement, and a focus on metrics. By staying adaptive to algorithm changes, fostering interaction, and enhancing searchability, you can increase your brand's visibility and reach across social platforms. As AI continues to shape social media experiences, maintaining an optimized presence ensures that your brand remains relevant, accessible, and engaging in an ever-evolving digital environment.

B. Managing Online Business Profiles

Maintaining accurate and engaging online business profiles is essential for maximizing visibility on search engines and improving local SEO. Platforms like *Google Business*

Profile and *Bing Places* play a crucial role in helping businesses appear in local search results, providing potential customers with key information about services, location, hours, and contact details. Properly managing these profiles enhances credibility, drives foot traffic, and establishes trust with online audiences. Here's how to optimize and manage business profiles on these major platforms to boost visibility and attract more customers.

1. Google Business Profile: Strengthening Local Presence on Google

Google Business Profile (GBP), formerly known as Google My Business, is one of the most influential tools for local SEO. GBP listings appear in Google's Local Pack, Google Maps, and local search results, making them invaluable for businesses looking to attract local customers.

- **How to Optimize Your Google Business Profile**:
    - **Ensure Complete and Accurate Information**: Fill out all fields, including business name, address, phone number, website, hours, and service categories. Accurate, consistent information helps Google understand your business and improves ranking in local search results.
    - **Use High-Quality Photos**: Adding photos of your business, products, or services can make your profile more engaging. Photos increase user interaction and make your listing more appealing in Google's visual results.
    - **Encourage and Respond to Reviews**: Customer reviews are a key ranking factor in Google's local algorithm. Encourage satisfied customers to leave positive reviews and respond to all feedback, as active engagement can boost your business's credibility and

visibility.
- **Use Google Posts to Share Updates**: Google Posts allow you to share timely updates, promotions, events, or new products directly in your GBP profile. Regular posts keep your listing active and can drive additional traffic and engagement.

2. Bing Places: Expanding Reach on Microsoft's Search Platform

While often overshadowed by Google, Bing Places remains important for businesses aiming to expand their reach. Bing serves a significant user base, and optimizing your Bing Places profile can help you capture traffic from Bing's local search results, as well as users on Microsoft-integrated devices and platforms.

- **How to Optimize Your Bing Places Profile**:
  - **Sync with Google Business Profile**: Bing Places allows you to sync your profile with Google Business Profile, which simplifies the process of updating information across platforms and ensures consistency between your listings.
  - **Add Relevant Business Categories and Attributes**: Selecting appropriate business categories helps Bing understand what your business offers and enhances relevance in search results. Add any special attributes that differentiate your business, such as wheelchair accessibility or pet-friendly policies.
  - **Incorporate Quality Images and Videos**: Adding images and videos to your Bing Places profile makes it more visually appealing. Include high-quality visuals that showcase your business's products, services, or location.

- **Leverage Bing's Customer Feedback Tools**: Bing Places allows you to manage customer reviews and ratings. Regularly monitoring and responding to reviews shows customer care and builds trust with potential clients browsing your listing.

3. Maintaining Consistency Across All Business Profiles

Consistency is key when managing online profiles across multiple platforms, as search engines prioritize businesses with accurate and uniform information. Discrepancies in business name, address, or phone number can create confusion and negatively impact SEO.

- **How to Maintain Consistency Across Profiles**:
    - **Use a Single Source of Truth for Information**: Keep a master document of all critical business information to ensure consistency across platforms. This includes your business name, address, phone number, website URL, hours, and service descriptions.
    - **Regularly Audit Listings**: Periodically check your listings on all platforms to ensure they remain accurate, especially if you change locations, contact details, or operating hours.
    - **Leverage Local Listing Management Tools**: Tools like Yext or Moz Local can simplify the process of managing and syncing business information across multiple directories, ensuring your data stays consistent and up-to-date.

Bringing It All Together: Building a Strong Local Profile Presence

Managing business profiles on platforms like Google Business Profile and Bing Places is essential for local SEO success and improved visibility in search engines. By keeping information accurate, encouraging customer reviews, and enhancing profiles with engaging visuals, you can establish a trustworthy online presence that attracts and converts local audiences. As more consumers rely on local search for immediate needs, a well-managed business profile becomes a crucial tool for driving in-person and online traffic, supporting both brand visibility and customer engagement.

C. Importance of Online Reviews and Ratings

Online reviews and ratings have become essential in shaping public perception and influencing decisions in local and AI-driven searches. Positive reviews not only boost a business's credibility but also play a significant role in improving local search rankings, as search engines prioritize businesses with strong reputations. In addition, AI-driven search platforms rely on user-generated reviews to gauge customer satisfaction, quality, and relevance, using this data to deliver better search results. Understanding the influence of reviews and ratings can help businesses build trust, attract new customers, and enhance visibility in an increasingly competitive digital environment.

1. Influence on Local Searches: Building Trust and Visibility

In local search results, businesses with high ratings and a solid number of positive reviews tend to rank higher, as search engines view these as indicators of quality and reliability. Google and Bing use reviews as a ranking factor for local SEO, displaying top-rated businesses prominently in the "Local Pack" or map results. Local customers often turn to these reviews to determine which businesses offer the best experiences, making it essential to foster a positive reputation.

- **How Reviews Impact Local Search Visibility**:
    - **Higher Ranking in Local Pack**: Google's Local Pack prioritizes businesses with positive reviews, high ratings, and active engagement. A well-rated business with recent reviews has a better chance of appearing in the top local search results.
    - **Increased Click-Through Rates (CTR)**: Listings with high ratings and a good volume of reviews are more likely to attract clicks, as users tend to trust businesses with proven track records.
    - **Strengthened Brand Reputation**: Consistently positive reviews build trust and credibility with local customers. A strong reputation can lead to more repeat business and recommendations, which further reinforces local visibility.

2. Influence on AI Searches: Enhancing Accuracy and User Satisfaction

AI-driven search platforms, including voice assistants, use online reviews to assess business quality and improve the accuracy of recommendations. Positive reviews signal to AI algorithms that a business consistently delivers quality, relevant experiences, making it more likely to be suggested when users ask for top-rated products or services. Ratings and reviews thus shape the responses of AI search platforms, influencing both visibility and customer trust.

- **How Reviews Impact AI-Driven Recommendations**:
    - **Priority in Voice-Activated Searches**: AI assistants like Siri, Alexa, and Google Assistant tend to prioritize businesses with high ratings and positive reviews when responding to local queries. For example, when a user asks for the "best pizza near me," voice assistants are likely to recommend the top-rated establishments based on review data.
    - **Improved Quality Signals for AI Algorithms**: AI algorithms use sentiment analysis to interpret the overall satisfaction reflected in reviews. High ratings combined with positive language increase the likelihood that a business will be featured in responses, particularly for questions about quality or experience.
    - **Increased User Trust in AI-Selected Results**: AI-driven searches are more effective when they deliver satisfying results to users. Positive reviews and high ratings enhance trust in the AI's recommendation, improving the user experience and reinforcing the business's reputation.

3. Encouraging and Managing Reviews: Strategies for Building a Strong Online Reputation

Proactively managing online reviews is essential for maintaining a strong reputation. Encouraging satisfied customers to leave reviews, responding to both positive and negative feedback, and regularly monitoring review platforms can help build and maintain credibility.

- **How to Encourage and Manage Reviews**:
    - **Request Reviews from Satisfied Customers**: Promptly ask satisfied customers to share their

experiences on major platforms like Google, Yelp, or Bing Places. Encourage feedback through follow-up emails, receipts, or customer service interactions.
- **Respond to All Reviews**: Engage with both positive and negative reviews to show that your business values customer feedback. Thank customers for positive reviews and address any concerns raised in negative reviews, demonstrating responsiveness and commitment to customer satisfaction.
- **Monitor and Learn from Feedback**: Regularly review feedback to identify patterns, strengths, and areas for improvement. Use constructive criticism to make adjustments to your offerings and continuously improve customer experience.

Bringing It All Together: The Power of Reviews in Local and AI Searches

Online reviews and ratings are vital for establishing trust, enhancing visibility, and improving local and AI-driven search rankings. Positive feedback not only attracts new customers but also strengthens a business's presence in local search results and AI recommendations. By actively encouraging and managing reviews, businesses can reinforce their reputation, increase customer satisfaction, and secure a competitive edge in both traditional and AI-driven search environments.

D. Content Distribution and Syndication

Content distribution and syndication are powerful strategies for extending a brand's reach and visibility across multiple platforms. By strategically sharing content on a variety of channels, businesses can engage new audiences, drive traffic back to their website, and enhance their SEO efforts. Whether it's through partnerships, social media, guest blogs, or content syndication networks, distributing content widely helps establish a brand as an industry authority, reinforces its message across platforms, and maximizes engagement. This section explores methods for effectively distributing and syndicating content to broaden your reach and solidify your online presence.

1. Social Media Platforms: Amplifying Content Through Audience Engagement

Social media remains one of the most effective channels for content distribution, allowing brands to reach diverse audiences and encourage real-time engagement. Sharing content across platforms like LinkedIn, Facebook, Twitter, and Instagram helps broaden visibility, while each channel's unique format allows for targeted messaging and creative adaptations of core content.

- **How to Optimize Content Distribution on Social Media**:
    - **Tailor Content to Each Platform**: Customize content for each social media platform to suit its audience and format. For instance, create visually engaging posts for Instagram, professional insights for LinkedIn, and concise updates for Twitter.
    - **Use Hashtags and Mentions**: Increase content discoverability by using relevant hashtags and mentioning industry influencers, partners, or clients where appropriate. This practice can boost engagement and potentially attract more followers.
    - **Schedule Regular Posts**: Maintain a consistent posting schedule to keep your audience engaged and ensure ongoing

visibility. Utilize social media scheduling tools like Hootsuite or Buffer to streamline the distribution process.

2. Guest Blogging and Partnerships: Leveraging External Platforms for Exposure

Collaborating with reputable websites and blogs through guest posts or partnerships can introduce your content to new audiences and build authority. Guest blogging provides valuable backlinks to your site, improves SEO, and reinforces your reputation as an industry expert.

- **How to Maximize Guest Blogging and Partnerships**:
    - **Identify High-Authority Sites**: Seek out well-regarded blogs and websites within your industry to host your content. High-authority sites improve backlink quality, boost your SEO, and lend credibility to your content.
    - **Align Content with Partner Audiences**: Craft content that is relevant and valuable to the partner's audience while remaining aligned with your brand's goals. This approach ensures greater engagement and adds value for readers.
    - **Include Author Bio and Links**: Add a brief author bio with links to your website or social media profiles, allowing interested readers to learn more and follow your brand. This is an effective way to drive traffic back to your website and expand your audience.

3. Content Syndication Networks: Expanding Reach Through Aggregators

Content syndication networks allow businesses to distribute their articles, blog posts, and other resources across multiple sites, enhancing exposure and reaching readers who may not encounter the content organically. Syndication platforms like Outbrain, Taboola, and Medium can be valuable for expanding reach and driving traffic back to your website.

- **How to Use Content Syndication Networks Effectively**:
    - **Choose Appropriate Syndication Platforms**: Select networks that align with your brand and audience. For example, Medium is well-suited for informative articles, while Outbrain and Taboola are often used for promotional or news content.
    - **Optimize Syndicated Content for Engagement**: Ensure that the syndicated content includes a strong headline, an engaging introduction, and clear calls-to-action to draw readers in and encourage them to explore further.
    - **Use Links Back to Your Site**: Incorporate backlinks within syndicated content to guide readers back to your site for more in-depth information. This drives traffic to your website and helps with lead generation and conversions.

4. Repurposing Content: Expanding Distribution Through Different Formats

Repurposing existing content into different formats, such

as infographics, videos, podcasts, or slide presentations, allows businesses to reach different segments of their audience across various platforms. This approach increases content longevity, enables multi-channel engagement, and provides opportunities for syndication in varied formats.

- **How to Repurpose Content for Broader Reach**:
    - **Transform Blogs into Videos or Infographics**: Visual content is highly shareable and appeals to users on platforms like YouTube and Pinterest. Converting a blog post into a video or infographic allows for wider distribution and engagement with visual learners.
    - **Create a Podcast Series or Audio Clips**: Audio content is increasingly popular, allowing users to engage with your brand on the go. Repurpose blog content or interviews into short podcast episodes to reach a new audience.
    - **Share Presentations on Slide Platforms**: Turn informative articles or reports into slides and share them on platforms like SlideShare, making complex topics digestible and accessible to presentation-focused audiences.

Bringing It All Together: Creating a Comprehensive Content Distribution Strategy

Expanding content reach through diverse channels—including social media, guest blogging, syndication networks, and repurposing—maximizes brand exposure and connects with audiences in varied formats. By strategically distributing content, businesses can attract new audiences, build credibility, and drive traffic back to their website, reinforcing a robust online presence.

Chapter 9. Leveraging Structured Data and Schema Markup

Structured data and schema markup are essential tools for helping search engines understand and categorize content more accurately. By adding structured data, businesses can improve how their content appears in search results, increasing visibility through rich snippets, enhanced listings, and other features that make search results more engaging and informative. Schema markup allows businesses to specify content details, such as product reviews, event dates, recipe ingredients, or FAQs, making it easier for search engines to present information directly in the search results.

A. Importance of Structured Data in AI SEO

Structured data is a critical component of modern SEO, especially as AI-driven search algorithms prioritize content that is clear, relevant, and easily accessible. Structured data helps search engines interpret the specific details of your content, enabling them to present it more effectively in search results through rich snippets, knowledge panels, and other enhanced listings. These enriched search features can increase click-through rates and user engagement, allowing businesses to capture attention directly from the search results page. As AI-powered search evolves, structured data becomes even more vital for delivering precise answers and enhancing visibility.

1. Enhancing Search Listings with Rich Snippets

Rich snippets are visually enhanced search results that include additional details such as ratings, images, prices, and other relevant information that appears directly beneath the meta description. Structured data is what powers these rich snippets, making it a valuable tool for increasing a search listing's appeal and relevance.

- **How Structured Data Powers Rich Snippets**:
    - **Schema Markup for Specific Content Types**: By using schema markup for various content types—such as recipes, products, reviews, or FAQs—businesses can signal to search engines exactly what their content entails. This structured format allows search engines to display data-rich elements, such as star ratings, cooking times, or event dates, right in the search results.
    - **Increased Visibility and Click-Through Rates**: Rich snippets make listings stand out in the search results, often leading to higher click-through rates. Users are more likely to click on listings that show relevant details upfront, as this added context helps them determine if the page will meet their needs.
    - **Improving Local Search Presence**: For businesses that rely on local search traffic, structured data can enhance visibility with details such as business hours, location, and contact information. LocalBusiness schema, for example, enables search engines to display these essential details, making it easier for potential customers to find and visit your business.

2. Leveraging Structured Data for AI-Driven Search Features

As AI-powered search platforms continue to integrate more advanced data interpretation techniques, structured data enables content to be better understood, sorted, and delivered to users based on specific needs or questions. Structured data plays a crucial role in allowing AI to pull specific answers or content segments, making it an essential optimization tool.

- **How AI Uses Structured Data in Search Features**:
    - **Supporting AI's Understanding of Content Context**: Structured data provides clear context about content types, which helps AI-driven search algorithms recognize and categorize the relevance of a page. For example, a "How-To" schema can improve the visibility of step-by-step guides, while a "Product" schema can better highlight an e-commerce item's details.
    - **Improving Content Accessibility in Voice Search**: Voice-activated search assistants rely on structured data to deliver precise, context-based answers. By adding schemas that fit the content's intent, such as FAQ, Recipe, or How-To, businesses can increase their chances of being selected by AI assistants for specific voice queries.
    - **Enabling Enhanced Display in Knowledge Panels**: Schema markup enables content to appear in knowledge panels, which display details about a person, brand, or business. This provides an authoritative way to present key information and improve brand visibility.

3. Types of Schema Markup to Implement for Rich Snippets and AI Optimization

Different types of schema markup can help tailor your content for rich snippets and AI-based search results. By selecting the right schema for your content type, you can maximize the chances of being featured in enhanced listings.

- **Essential Schema Types for SEO**:
    - **FAQ Schema**: Ideal for common questions, FAQ schema can help content appear in Google's expanded Q&A results, providing users with direct answers.
    - **Product and Review Schema**: These schemas are valuable for e-commerce, enabling search engines to showcase product details, ratings, and prices. This is particularly helpful for users who rely on AI search platforms for product comparisons and recommendations.
    - **How-To Schema**: This markup is useful for tutorials, guiding users through step-by-step processes. How-To schema can improve visibility in searches related to specific instructions, making it a popular choice for instructional content.
    - **LocalBusiness Schema**: Essential for local SEO, this schema displays business hours, locations, contact information, and other pertinent details, helping AI platforms provide accurate local results.

Bringing It All Together: Structured Data as a Foundation for AI SEO

Structured data and schema markup are foundational for optimizing content. By providing search engines with well-organized, structured information, businesses can ensure their content is displayed accurately and attractively through rich snippets and other AI-driven search features. Implementing structured data not only enhances visibility but also aligns content with the specific needs of AI algorithms, ensuring that your brand remains relevant, discoverable, and user-focused as search technology advances.

B. Types of Schema Markup

Schema markup is a powerful tool for structuring data on your website, helping search engines interpret and display content in enhanced formats like rich snippets, knowledge panels, and more. Using the right types of schema markup enables businesses to improve visibility, boost click-through rates, and better serve user intent directly in search results. Here's a breakdown of some of the most valuable schema types—*Organization, Product, Review, FAQ,* and *How-To*—and how each can support SEO efforts by improving the way content is presented in search results.

1. Organization Schema: Establishing Brand Presence and Authority

The Organization schema markup is essential for businesses and organizations looking to establish a strong brand presence in search results. This schema allows search engines to display key organizational details, such as a company's logo, contact information, social media profiles, and address. Organization schema helps businesses appear more authoritative and trustworthy, which can enhance brand visibility in search results and knowledge panels.

- **Key Attributes**:
    - **Organization Name and Logo**: Display your organization's official name and logo to improve brand recognition in search results.
    - **Contact Information**: Add a phone number, email, or other contact details to make it easier for users to reach you directly from the search page.

- **Social Media Profiles**: Linking social profiles helps strengthen brand identity and allows users to connect with your business on other platforms.

- **SEO Benefits**: Organization schema improves brand authority, ensures accurate display of business information, and enhances the appearance of your brand in knowledge panels.

2. Product Schema: Optimizing for E-Commerce Visibility

Product schema markup is particularly valuable for e-commerce sites, as it enables search engines to display product-specific details like pricing, availability, and images directly in search results. This schema is essential for businesses that want their products to stand out and attract high-intent shoppers, as these rich snippets allow users to make informed purchasing decisions quickly.

- **Key Attributes**:
    - **Product Name and Description**: Clearly present your product's name and a concise description to attract users.
    - **Price and Availability**: Displaying price and availability (e.g., "In Stock" or "Out of Stock") provides essential information that can influence buying decisions.
    - **Product Image**: High-quality product images in search results help create a visually appealing snippet that can increase clicks.

- **SEO Benefits**: Product schema makes product listings more informative and engaging, increasing the likelihood of appearing in shopping-related searches and driving higher click-through rates.

3. Review Schema: Enhancing Trust with Ratings and Testimonials

Review schema allows businesses to showcase customer reviews and ratings directly in search results, creating social proof that can improve credibility and attract more clicks. Displaying ratings in search snippets helps build trust with potential customers, as users often rely on reviews when making purchase decisions.

- **Key Attributes**:
    - **Aggregate Rating**: Present an average rating score from multiple reviews, often displayed as star ratings, to give users an at-a-glance idea of your product's quality.
    - **Individual Reviews**: Highlight specific customer reviews or testimonials that provide more context about the product or service.
    - **Review Count**: Including the number of reviews lends credibility to the average rating and helps users gauge the popularity of the product or service.

- **SEO Benefits**: Review schema boosts credibility, attracts user attention through star ratings in search results, and can improve conversions by leveraging social proof.

4. FAQ Schema: Answering Common Questions Directly in Search Results

FAQ schema is an effective tool for addressing common questions directly on the search results page. When implemented correctly, this markup can expand your search snippet to include frequently asked questions and answers, allowing users to get immediate insights into your offerings.

- **Key Attributes**:
    - **Question and Answer Pairs**: Each question is paired with a direct, concise answer that gives users quick access to information.
    - **Relevant and Informative Answers**: Ensure that answers are accurate and relevant to user queries, as search engines prioritize content that provides clear, helpful responses.
- **SEO Benefits**: FAQ schema increases the real estate of your listing in search results, improves user engagement, and positions your content as a go-to resource for commonly asked questions.

5. How-To Schema: Guiding Users with Step-by-Step Instructions

The How-To schema is ideal for content that provides instructional guidance, such as DIY projects, recipes, or tutorials. This markup allows search engines to display step-by-step instructions in a structured format, making it easier for users to follow along. How-To schema is particularly useful for mobile and voice searches, where users are often looking for quick and clear directions.

- **Key Attributes**:
    - **Steps and Descriptions**: Break down each step with a brief description, creating a clear path for users to follow.
    - **Visual Aids (Optional)**: Adding images or videos for each step enhances the instructional value and makes it more engaging.
    - **Estimated Time and Tools**: For relevant topics, include details on how long the process takes or any required tools/materials.
- **SEO Benefits**: How-To schema increases visibility

for instructional content, makes search results more interactive, and improves user experience by delivering step-by-step guides directly on the search page.

Bringing It All Together: Selecting Schema Markup for Maximum SEO Impact

By implementing Organization, Product, Review, FAQ, and How-To schema markup, businesses can ensure that their content is well-structured, relevant, and accessible for search engines to display in enhanced formats. These schema types allow for richer, more engaging search results, improving visibility and user engagement across a variety of search intents. Leveraging schema markup as part of your SEO strategy helps establish authority, attract clicks, and ultimately meet users' needs in a more direct, informative way.

C. Implementing Structured Data Correctly

Implementing structured data correctly is essential for ensuring that search engines can accurately interpret and display your content in enhanced formats like rich snippets, knowledge panels, and featured snippets. When done well, structured data can improve your content's visibility and engagement; however, common mistakes can prevent schema from working effectively or even lead to penalties. Following best practices helps optimize your schema markup for search engines while avoiding errors that can hinder your SEO efforts. Here's a guide to best practices and common pitfalls to watch for when implementing structured data.

1. Best Practices for Structured Data Implementation

Correctly implementing structured data requires careful planning, consistent application, and regular validation to ensure your schema remains accurate and up-to-date. By following these best practices, you can maximize the SEO benefits of structured data and enhance your content's search visibility.

- **Use Schema.org Markup Types**: Schema.org is the most widely supported standard for structured data. Choose schema types that align with your content, such as Product, Review, FAQ, and How-To, to ensure accurate categorization. The Schema.org library provides detailed descriptions and properties for each type, which helps guide you in selecting and applying the right markup.

- **Test Your Structured Data**: Regularly validate your schema with tools like Google's Rich Results Test and the Schema Markup Validator to ensure it is functioning correctly. Testing structured data allows you to catch and fix any errors before they impact search visibility.

- **Place JSON-LD in the <head> or <body> Tags**: JSON-LD (JavaScript Object Notation for Linked Data) is the recommended format for structured data because it's easy to implement and does not disrupt your HTML. Place JSON-LD code within the <head> or <body> tags to ensure search engines can easily access and process it.

- **Focus on Relevance and Accuracy**: Ensure that your structured data accurately represents the content on the page. For example, if you're marking up a product page, only include product-related schema rather than irrelevant types. Accurate schema helps search engines display relevant information and improves the chances of earning rich snippets.

- **Update Schema Regularly**: If your content changes—such as updating product prices, availability, or event dates—make sure to update your schema to reflect these changes. Consistent updates help maintain the accuracy and reliability of your structured data.

2. Common Mistakes to Avoid with Structured Data

Avoiding common mistakes when implementing structured data is crucial to prevent errors, penalties, or loss of visibility. Below are some pitfalls that can hinder the effectiveness of your schema markup.

- **Overloading with Irrelevant Schema**: Using too many schema types that don't apply to the content can confuse search engines and dilute the effectiveness of your markup. Stick to schema types that match the primary content of the page to keep the focus clear and relevant.

- **Using Incorrect Schema Types**: Choosing the wrong schema type for your content can prevent it from displaying correctly in search results. For instance, using Recipe schema for a blog post that isn't a recipe can mislead search engines and reduce your chances of gaining rich snippets. Always ensure the schema type aligns with the content's intent.

- **Leaving Out Required or Recommended Properties**: Each schema type has required and recommended properties (such as name, description, and price for Product schema). Failing to include these can prevent the schema from working correctly.

Refer to Schema.org documentation to ensure you're including the right properties for each type.

- **Marking Up Hidden or Inaccurate Content**: Google and other search engines may penalize sites that use structured data for content that isn't visible to users. Only apply schema to visible, accurate content that aligns with what users see on the page. Avoid adding structured data for content that doesn't match the page's purpose or intent.

- **Neglecting to Monitor and Update Structured Data**: Structured data can become outdated if you change the content but forget to update the markup. Regularly audit and update structured data, especially for time-sensitive content like events, prices, and availability.

- **Ignoring Google's Structured Data Guidelines**: Google has specific guidelines for structured data, and failing to follow them can result in manual actions or penalties. Review Google's guidelines to ensure your schema meets search engine requirements and aligns with best practices.

3. Tools for Structured Data Implementation and Validation

Using the right tools helps simplify the implementation and validation of structured data, making it easier to identify and correct issues.

- **Google's Rich Results Test**: This tool tests whether your structured data is eligible for rich results and shows any errors or warnings that may affect visibility.

- **Schema Markup Validator**: This validator from Schema.org checks for compliance with schema standards, allowing you to verify if your structured data is implemented correctly.

- **Google Search Console**: The "Enhancements" report in Search Console highlights any structured data errors and provides insights on how your schema is performing in search results.

Bringing It All Together: Implementing Structured Data for Maximum SEO Impact

Implementing structured data correctly is essential for maximizing its benefits, from enhanced visibility to improved user experience. By following best practices, regularly testing and updating schema, and avoiding common mistakes, you can ensure that your structured data aligns with search engine requirements and boosts your SEO strategy. A well-implemented structured data strategy not only helps search engines understand your content but also enhances your presence in search results, making it a valuable asset.

D. Testing and Validating Structured Data

Testing and validating structured data is crucial for ensuring that search engines can correctly interpret and display your content in enhanced formats like rich snippets, knowledge panels, and other rich results. Google's *Rich Results Test* is a valuable tool that allows you to check if your structured data is eligible for rich results, identify any errors or warnings, and verify that your schema markup aligns with Google's requirements. Regular testing and validation of structured data helps maintain its effectiveness and prevents issues that could impact your visibility in search results.

1. Using Google's Rich Results Test: Ensuring Schema Eligibility

Google's Rich Results Test is designed to analyze structured data and determine if it meets the requirements for rich results. This tool allows you to test individual pages or pieces of structured data and provides feedback on potential issues. Testing ensures that your markup is functioning as intended and aligns with Google's guidelines.

- **How to Use the Rich Results Test**:
    - **Enter the URL or Code**: You can either enter the URL of the page you want to test or paste the structured data code directly into the tool. This flexibility allows you to test live pages or preview code snippets before they go live.
    - **Run the Test**: Once you enter the URL or code, run the test. Google's tool will analyze the structured data and check for eligibility for rich results, such as FAQs, recipes, products, or events.
    - **Review Results for Errors and Warnings**: The test provides a report highlighting any errors or warnings in the structured data. Errors are critical issues that prevent rich result eligibility, while warnings indicate optional enhancements that could improve the data but are not mandatory.

- **Best Practices for Testing Structured Data**:
    - **Fix Errors Immediately**: Errors will prevent your structured data from generating rich results, so it's essential to address them promptly. Correcting errors can improve your eligibility for enhanced search features.
    - **Consider Warnings as Optimization**

Opportunities: While warnings don't prevent rich results, they provide suggestions for additional properties that can make your structured data more comprehensive. Addressing warnings can enhance the data's quality and improve user engagement.
- **Test Regularly**: Regularly test structured data, especially after making content updates or schema changes. Frequent testing helps catch issues early and ensures that your structured data remains up-to-date.

2. Additional Tools for Structured Data Validation

While Google's Rich Results Test is highly effective, using multiple validation tools can give a more comprehensive view of your structured data's performance and compatibility with various search engines. Below are additional tools that complement the Rich Results Test:

- **Schema Markup Validator (Schema.org)**: This tool, provided by Schema.org, checks your structured data against schema standards. It's useful for verifying if your markup complies with the Schema.org vocabulary and for identifying syntax issues that may not appear in Google's tool.

- **Google Search Console**: The "Enhancements" report in Google Search Console provides insights on how your structured data is performing and highlights any issues detected over time. It also tracks how often your site appears in search results with rich features, allowing you to monitor schema impact.

- **Bing Webmaster Tools**: Bing Webmaster Tools offers structured data validation and can help you ensure your schema is compatible with Bing's requirements, extending your reach across multiple search engines.

3. Common Issues in Structured Data Validation and How to Fix Them

Structured data errors can prevent content from displaying as rich results, while warnings may limit the quality of the information presented. Understanding common issues in validation and how to resolve them is essential.

- **Missing Required Properties**: Structured data types often have required properties that must be included for the schema to function properly. If a required property, such as "name" or "datePublished" for an article, is missing, add it to ensure the schema is complete.

- **Incorrect or Unsupported Schema Types**: Using the wrong schema type for content can lead to issues. For example, marking a general blog post with Product schema may confuse search engines. Always choose schema types that match the content's purpose and intended use.

- **Outdated or Inconsistent Information**: Structured data should be updated regularly, especially for details like prices, product availability, or event dates. Inconsistent information can affect credibility and user experience, so keep all data accurate and current.

Bringing It All Together: Ensuring Effective Structured Data with Regular Testing

Testing and validating structured data through tools like Google's Rich Results Test is essential for maximizing the effectiveness of schema markup. Regular testing, error correction, and attention to warnings help maintain eligibility for rich results and improve user engagement with enhanced listings. By incorporating structured data validation into your SEO routine, you can ensure that your content is accurately represented in search results and continues to support your overall digital visibility and engagement goals.

Chapter 10. Content Strategy in the Age of AI

As artificial intelligence becomes a central component of search engines and digital platforms, content strategy must evolve to meet the demands of AI-driven algorithms, personalization, and new user behaviors. AI has reshaped how search engines interpret content, prioritize relevance, and present results, emphasizing the importance of context, intent, and user engagement. An effective content strategy in the age of AI prioritizes high-quality, contextually relevant content that resonates with users and aligns with AI's analytical capabilities.

A. Developing an AI-Optimized Content Plan

Creating a content plan that aligns with both user intent and AI-driven preferences is essential for maintaining visibility and relevance. AI-powered algorithms are increasingly capable of interpreting content in context, analyzing user intent, and assessing engagement patterns. As a result, a successful content plan must focus on delivering value through relevant, intent-driven content that meets the needs of users and leverages AI's analytical strengths. Here's how to develop an AI-optimized content plan that resonates with users while enhancing search performance.

1. Aligning Content with User Intent

User intent is at the core of AI-powered search, as search engines strive to deliver results that directly address the specific needs and queries of users. To create content that aligns with different types of user intent—informational, navigational, transactional, and commercial—businesses must understand the underlying motivations behind each search and tailor their content accordingly.

- **Types of User Intent**:
    - **Informational Intent**: Users seek knowledge on a topic (e.g., "how to start a vegetable garden"). Content for informational intent should be comprehensive, detailed, and educational, providing clear answers and value.
    - **Navigational Intent**: Users aim to reach a specific page or site (e.g., "LinkedIn login"). Content for navigational queries should ensure that brand pages are optimized for visibility and easy navigation.
    - **Transactional Intent**: Users are ready to make a purchase or take action (e.g., "buy electric lawn mower"). Transactional content should be persuasive, product-focused, and include clear calls-to-action, such as product pages and service descriptions.
    - **Commercial Investigation Intent**: Users are comparing options before a decision (e.g., "best smartphones 2024"). Content targeting this intent should focus on comparison guides, reviews, and case studies that help users make informed choices.

- **How to Align Content with Intent**:
    - **Conduct Intent-Focused Keyword Research**: Use keyword tools to identify terms associated with each intent type. Tools like SEMrush, Ahrefs, or Answer the Public can help identify popular queries for various stages of the user journey.
    - **Structure Content for Quick Answers**: Format content with headings, lists, and bullet points to address specific questions clearly and directly, increasing chances of being selected for rich snippets or featured snippets.
    - **Monitor Intent Shifts**: Regularly analyze search trends to stay updated on shifts in

user intent within your industry. For example, informational searches may increase during seasonal trends, while transactional intent may peak around holidays.

2. Optimizing for AI-Driven Content Preferences

AI algorithms prioritize content that demonstrates relevance, authority, and engagement. An AI-optimized content plan must incorporate elements that enhance these qualities, ensuring that content not only ranks well but also resonates with users.

- **Content Quality and Depth**: AI-driven search algorithms favor in-depth, well-researched content that thoroughly covers a topic. High-quality content that provides unique insights, data, or perspectives is more likely to be favored by AI algorithms.
    - **Create Comprehensive Guides**: Long-form content or in-depth guides that address a topic thoroughly help establish authority and engage users for longer periods, which can improve rankings.
    - **Use Data and Visuals**: Incorporating data, infographics, and visuals not only adds value but also aligns with AI's preference for structured and multimedia-rich content.

- **E-E-A-T (Experience, Expertise, Authority, Trust)**: AI algorithms assess content for E-E-A-T qualities, emphasizing the importance of expertise and trustworthiness in content creation.
    - **Showcase Author Expertise**: Display author credentials, experience, or certifications to demonstrate authority. Content written by industry experts is more likely to rank well, especially in fields like finance, health, and law.

- o **Include Trust Signals**: Use external links to reputable sources, cite studies or research, and add customer testimonials to enhance credibility.

- **Engagement and User Signals**: AI-driven search engines analyze engagement metrics, such as click-through rate (CTR), dwell time, and bounce rate, to assess user satisfaction.
  - o **Focus on User-Centric Headlines and Intros**: Create compelling headlines and introductions that capture attention and encourage clicks. Strong opening paragraphs help reduce bounce rate by quickly establishing relevance.
  - o **Enhance Readability**: Use short paragraphs, bullet points, and clear subheadings to improve readability. AI favors content that is easy to consume and engages users throughout.

3. Integrating Data & Personalization in Content Strategy

AI algorithms thrive on data, and using data insights to personalize content can help ensure that your content resonates with users on a deeper level. Personalization, based on factors such as user location, behavior, and preferences, can make your content more relevant and engaging.

- **Use Analytics to Inform Content Creation**: Regularly analyze data from Google Analytics, social media insights, and other tools to identify user preferences and content performance. Determine which topics, formats, and keywords resonate most with your audience.

- **Create Audience Segments**: Divide your target

audience into segments based on demographics, interests, or purchase behavior. Use these segments to tailor content to specific needs, enhancing relevancy and user satisfaction.

- **Leverage Dynamic Content and Localized Keywords**: Personalize content for different locations and contexts using localized keywords and dynamic content elements. AI algorithms prioritize content that reflects user-specific interests, such as local events or product availability.

Bringing It All Together: Building an AI-Optimized Content Plan

An AI-optimized content plan is a strategic approach that balances user intent, AI-driven preferences, and data-driven insights to create content that is relevant, authoritative, and engaging. By aligning content with intent, prioritizing quality, and leveraging personalization, businesses can create a comprehensive content plan that enhances visibility, improves engagement, and maintains competitiveness.

B. Creating Conversational and Engaging Content

In an era where AI-driven algorithms value natural language and user-centric content, creating conversational and engaging content has become essential. Content that feels approachable and interactive not only captures users' attention but also improves engagement metrics like dwell time, shares, and user satisfaction, all of which are key for SEO. Using storytelling techniques and encouraging user interaction are powerful ways to create a conversational tone that resonates with audiences and aligns with AI's preference for meaningful, engaging content. Here's how to craft conversational and engaging content through storytelling and interactive elements.

1. Using Storytelling Techniques to Connect with Audiences

Storytelling has always been a way to connect with audiences, making information memorable, relatable, and engaging. In content marketing, effective storytelling transforms information into a compelling narrative that draws users in and makes content more enjoyable.

- **Start with a Strong Hook**: Capturing attention from the first sentence is crucial. Use a question, an interesting fact, or a relatable scenario to draw readers in. For example, "Have you ever wondered why some brands feel like friends, while others feel distant?"

- **Develop a Relatable Narrative**: Frame information in a way that resonates with your audience's experiences or challenges. For instance, instead of simply describing a product's features, share a story about how it solved a problem for a customer. This approach helps users see themselves in the narrative, creating a personal connection.

- **Incorporate Emotions and Sensory Details**: Engaging content taps into emotions, making readers feel connected. Use sensory details, metaphors, or analogies to create vivid imagery, whether it's the satisfaction of a job well done or the excitement of discovering something new. This emotional resonance can make content more impactful.

- **Conclude with a Takeaway or Call-to-Action (CTA)**: End stories with a clear message, takeaway, or CTA. Whether it's a moral, a lesson, or an invitation to take action, a strong conclusion helps reinforce the story's purpose and encourages readers to engage further.

2. Encouraging User Interaction for an Engaging Experience

Interactive content invites users to participate, turning passive readers into active participants. AI-driven algorithms favor engaging content that keeps users on the page longer, and interactive elements—such as questions, polls, and comments—create opportunities for real-time user engagement.

- **Use Conversational Language and Questions**: Address the reader directly, using "you" to make the content feel more personal. Pose questions throughout the text to create a two-way conversation, such as "Have you experienced this problem before?" or "What would you do in this situation?" This encourages readers to think about the content and engage more deeply.

- **Include Interactive Elements like Polls and Quizzes**: Embedding polls, quizzes, or interactive graphics allows readers to participate and learn more actively. For instance, an article on eco-friendly practices might include a quiz titled, "How Sustainable Are Your Habits?" These elements make the content experience more dynamic and memorable.

- **Encourage Comments and Discussions**: Prompt readers to leave comments by asking open-ended questions at the end of your content, such as "What's your biggest challenge in this area?" or "Share your thoughts below!" Comments add user-generated content to your page, enhancing its value for both users and search engines.

- **Embed Multimedia Content**: Videos, infographics, and image galleries offer a visual break and keep users engaged. Embedding multimedia within the content helps illustrate points visually and provides an interactive, multi-dimensional experience.

3. Adopting a Conversational Tone to Enhance Readability and Relatability

A conversational tone helps content feel approachable and authentic, making it easier for users to relate to the message. This tone is particularly effective in blog posts, guides, and FAQ sections, where a relaxed style keeps readers comfortable and engaged.

- **Write in Short Sentences and Paragraphs**: Break content into digestible chunks to improve readability. Short sentences and paragraphs create a more conversational rhythm that feels natural and accessible.

- **Use Simple, Everyday Language**: Avoid jargon and complex terminology whenever possible. AI-driven algorithms favor content that's accessible to a wide audience, and clear language improves both readability and comprehension.

- **Share Personal Insights or Experiences**: Personal anecdotes or insights add authenticity and humanize the content. For instance, in a guide about productivity, a relatable comment like "I used to struggle with staying focused too" can build rapport and make the content feel more genuine.

Bringing It All Together: Engaging Audiences with

Conversational and Interactive Content

Creating conversational and engaging content requires a balance of storytelling, interactivity, and readability. By incorporating relatable narratives, encouraging interaction, and adopting a conversational tone, businesses can build a stronger connection with their audience and improve engagement metrics that AI algorithms prioritize. As content continues to play a vital role in search visibility and user satisfaction, using these techniques will help ensure that your content remains both captivating and valuable.

C. Utilizing AI Tools for Content Creation

In the age of AI, content creators have access to powerful tools that enhance productivity, improve content quality, and provide valuable insights into audience preferences. AI writing assistants and content analysis tools streamline the creation process by generating content ideas, optimizing text, and analyzing engagement metrics. By leveraging these tools, businesses can produce high-quality, targeted content faster, helping to meet the demands of AI-driven search algorithms and user expectations. Here's how to use AI writing assistants and content analysis tools effectively within your content strategy.

1. AI Writing Assistants: Boosting Efficiency and Creativity

AI writing assistants like ChatGPT, Jasper, and Copy.ai offer capabilities that range from drafting content to enhancing readability, making them valuable tools for brainstorming and accelerating the writing process. While these tools don't replace human creativity, they provide structure, inspiration, and editing support, allowing content creators to focus on refining the message and tone.

- **Generating Content Ideas and Outlines**: AI writing assistants can help generate ideas based on topic prompts, identify trending themes, and even create outlines for blog posts, articles, and social media content. For example, a prompt like "tips for eco-friendly living" might generate a list of actionable tips that serve as the basis for a detailed article.

- **Creating Initial Drafts**: AI tools can produce drafts quickly, providing a foundation for writers to build upon. By creating an initial version, AI helps reduce the time spent on drafting, allowing writers to concentrate on fine-tuning and adding unique insights.

- **Enhancing Readability and Tone**: AI tools like Grammarly and Hemingway Editor offer readability enhancements, grammar checks, and tone suggestions. They help ensure that content is clear, concise, and suited to the intended audience, making it easier for readers to engage and comprehend.

- **Optimizing Content for SEO**: Some AI writing tools provide keyword recommendations and can integrate SEO elements directly into the content. Platforms like Clearscope and SurferSEO analyze search intent and suggest keywords or phrases that enhance relevance, making the content more likely to rank in search results.

2. Content Analysis Tools: Measuring Performance and Optimizing Content

Content analysis tools provide valuable insights into how content performs and resonates with audiences. By examining metrics like engagement, readability, and keyword relevance, these tools allow content creators to optimize based on real data. AI-driven analytics can reveal patterns in user behavior and guide adjustments to improve reach, engagement, and conversion rates.

- **Understanding Audience Engagement**: Tools like Google Analytics, BuzzSumo, and SEMrush analyze metrics like page views, time on page, bounce rates, and social shares. These insights help content creators identify what works well and which areas need improvement. For example, high bounce rates may indicate that content isn't matching user intent, while high engagement rates suggest it's hitting the mark.

- **Conducting Topic and Competitor Analysis**: AI-powered analysis tools can track trending topics within your industry, revealing high-performing keywords and popular content themes. Competitor analysis through platforms like Ahrefs or BuzzSumo offers insights into what types of content resonate with similar audiences, helping refine your own content strategy.

- **Optimizing Content Readability and Structure**: Readability scores, such as those from tools like Yoast or Hemingway, help ensure that content is accessible to a broad audience. These tools can highlight complex sentences or jargon, making it easier to adjust and enhance clarity. Content structured for readability not only performs better with users but also aligns with AI algorithms that prioritize user-friendly formats.

- **Tracking SEO and Keyword Performance**: Platforms like SEMrush, Moz, and Ahrefs provide keyword rankings, backlink data, and site performance metrics. These insights are essential for understanding how your content is performing in search results and for refining your SEO strategy. Regular keyword performance tracking helps you adjust content over time to maintain or improve rankings.

3. Integrating AI Tools for a Cohesive Content Creation Workflow

To maximize the benefits of AI in content creation, it's essential to integrate AI writing assistants and content analysis tools into a cohesive workflow. This approach allows content teams to streamline planning, drafting, analyzing, and optimizing processes for efficient and data-driven content production.

- **Plan and Brainstorm with AI**: Use AI writing tools to generate topic ideas, research trending keywords, and outline content. AI can speed up brainstorming sessions, helping to focus on high-potential topics from the start.

- **Draft and Edit with AI Assistance**: Create initial drafts using AI writing assistants, then refine the content manually to add unique insights, storytelling elements, and a personalized tone. Use grammar and readability tools to polish the text and ensure it aligns with brand standards.

- **Analyze and Adjust Based on AI Insights**: After publishing, use content analysis tools to monitor performance and engagement metrics. AI-driven insights from analytics platforms can guide updates, identify high-performing content, and inform future content topics.

Bringing It All Together: Leveraging AI Tools for Enhanced Content Strategy

AI writing assistants and content analysis tools have become indispensable in modern content strategy, enabling teams to produce engaging, SEO-friendly content more efficiently. By combining AI-assisted creation with real-time data analysis, businesses can refine their approach, making content that resonates with audiences and aligns with AI-driven search preferences. Integrating these tools into your workflow not only improves productivity but also enhances the quality, reach, and impact of your content.

D. Monitoring Content Performance

To maintain a successful content strategy in the age of AI, it's essential to continuously monitor and evaluate content performance. Tracking metrics like engagement, conversion rates, and user satisfaction allows businesses to optimize their content based on data-driven insights. Through analytics, A/B testing, and user feedback, brands can refine their content strategy to better meet user intent, improve visibility, and boost engagement. Here's how to use these tools and techniques to monitor and enhance content performance effectively.

1. Analytics: Understanding Key Metrics and Insights

Analytics tools provide a wealth of data that helps measure how well content is performing. By examining metrics like page views, bounce rate, time on page, and conversion rates, businesses can determine which content resonates most with audiences and identify areas for improvement.

- **Tools for Content Analytics**:
    - **Google Analytics**: A foundational tool for monitoring web traffic, user behavior, and conversion metrics. Use Google Analytics to analyze page views, session duration, user

flow, and conversion tracking, gaining insights into how users interact with your content.
- **Social Media Analytics**: Platforms like Facebook Insights, Twitter Analytics, and LinkedIn Analytics offer engagement metrics specific to social media. Monitoring likes, shares, comments, and impressions helps assess the impact of social media content and adjust strategies accordingly.
- **SEO Tools (e.g., Ahrefs, SEMrush)**: These tools provide keyword rankings, backlinks, and traffic insights, helping you monitor how your content performs in search results and identify opportunities for optimization.

- **Key Metrics to Track**:
  - **Engagement Metrics**: Time on page, scroll depth, and click-through rates indicate how engaging and relevant your content is to users.
  - **Bounce Rate**: A high bounce rate may signal that content isn't meeting user intent, while a low bounce rate suggests that users find the content valuable and are staying longer.
  - **Conversion Rate**: Tracking conversion goals, such as sign-ups, downloads, or purchases, helps assess how effectively your content drives user action.

2. A/B Testing: Experimenting for Improved Content Performance

A/B testing allows businesses to experiment with different versions of content to determine which elements resonate most with audiences. By testing variables like headlines, images, call-to-action (CTA) buttons, or content layouts, you can identify what drives engagement and conversions.

- **How to Conduct A/B Testing**:
    - **Select Variables to Test**: Choose one element to test at a time, such as the headline, CTA wording, or image placement. Testing too many variables at once can make it difficult to isolate which change influenced the results.
    - **Run Tests on a Representative Audience**: Use A/B testing platforms like Google Optimize, Optimizely, or HubSpot to split your audience evenly between two versions of the content. Ensure that the sample size is large enough for statistically significant results.
    - **Analyze Results and Implement Changes**: Compare performance metrics for each version, such as click-through rates or conversion rates. Implement the version that performs best, and consider additional tests to further refine content.

- **Elements to A/B Test**:
    - **Headlines and Titles**: Test different headlines to see which version attracts more clicks and engagement. Clear, compelling headlines should improve traffic and click-through rates.
    - **CTA Placement and Wording**: Experiment with CTA buttons or links to determine the most effective position and wording. Even small changes, like switching "Learn More" to "Get Started," can impact conversions.
    - **Content Layout and Visuals**: Test content layout, such as paragraph length, image placement, and bullet points, to improve readability and user engagement.

3. User Feedback: Gathering Direct Insights from Your Audience

User feedback is an invaluable tool for understanding how real users perceive and interact with your content. By collecting direct feedback, businesses can make data-informed adjustments that enhance content relevance, usability, and satisfaction.

- **Methods for Collecting User Feedback**:
    - **Surveys and Polls**: Use surveys to ask users about their experience with your content. Tools like SurveyMonkey, Google Forms, and in-platform polls (e.g., LinkedIn or Instagram) can help gather feedback on specific content pieces or general preferences.
    - **Comment Sections and Social Media Engagement**: Comments and social media interactions offer insights into user reactions and preferences. Analyze common themes in comments or replies to identify areas for improvement or new content ideas.
    - **Customer Support and Chat Feedback**: If your website has a live chat feature or customer support channels, these interactions can provide valuable feedback on content-related questions or pain points. Use this information to address gaps in your content or create FAQs and guides.

- **Types of Feedback to Collect**:
    - **Content Relevance and Quality**: Ask users if they found the content helpful, informative, and relevant to their needs. Direct feedback on quality can reveal insights that analytics alone may not provide.
    - **Usability and Navigation**: Inquire about ease of navigation, readability, and whether users found the content format engaging. This feedback can guide improvements in layout and design.

- **Topics and Suggestions**: Encourage users to suggest topics or ask questions. Knowing what your audience wants to read can help you plan future content that aligns with their interests.

Bringing It All Together: A Comprehensive Approach to Content Monitoring

Monitoring content performance through analytics, A/B testing, and user feedback provides a holistic understanding of what works, what doesn't, and where opportunities for improvement lie. By integrating data-driven insights with real user feedback, businesses can refine their content strategy, improve user satisfaction, and continuously optimize for engagement and conversions. Consistently evaluating and adjusting content ensures it remains relevant, valuable, and impactful for your audience.

Chapter 11. Technical SEO Enhancements for the AI Era

In the AI-driven era, technical SEO has evolved beyond traditional practices to include advanced strategies that improve how search engines interpret, crawl, and rank content. AI algorithms prioritize not only content quality but also page performance, accessibility, and the structure of a website, making technical SEO essential for maintaining strong visibility. Optimizing for fast load times, mobile-friendliness, structured data, and enhanced user experience signals ensures that your site is fully aligned with AI-powered search engines' requirements.

A. Site Speed Optimization Techniques

In the AI-driven era, site speed is more critical than ever, as fast-loading pages provide a better user experience and align with search engines' emphasis on performance. Google's Core Web Vitals, for instance, prioritize metrics like loading speed, interactivity, and visual stability, making speed a crucial ranking factor. Slow load times can increase bounce rates, reduce engagement, and negatively impact rankings. By optimizing site speed through techniques such as image compression, code minification, and CDN usage, you can improve user satisfaction and maintain visibility in search results. Here's how to enhance site speed using these essential methods.

1. Image Compression: Reducing File Sizes for Faster Loading

Images often account for a significant portion of a page's

load time. Compressing images reduces their file size without compromising quality, helping to speed up page loading and improve user experience. Image compression techniques are especially beneficial for visually rich sites, such as e-commerce stores and blogs.

- **How to Compress Images**:
    - **Choose Optimal File Formats**: Use efficient formats like JPEG or WebP for photographs and PNG for images that require transparency. WebP, in particular, offers high quality with smaller file sizes.
    - **Use Compression Tools**: Tools like TinyPNG, JPEG-Optimizer, or online compressors like Squoosh can significantly reduce image file sizes. For bulk optimization, plugins like Smush for WordPress automatically compress images upon upload.
    - **Implement Lazy Loading**: Lazy loading defers the loading of off-screen images until the user scrolls to them, reducing the initial load time. Most major CMS platforms offer plugins or settings to enable lazy loading.

- **Best Practices**:
    - **Set Maximum Dimensions**: Limit image dimensions based on your site's layout to prevent unnecessarily large images from slowing down load times.
    - **Optimize Alt Text and Captions**: While not directly related to speed, adding alt text improves accessibility and SEO without increasing file size.

2. Code Minification: Reducing JavaScript, CSS, and HTML File Sizes

Code minification involves removing unnecessary characters, spaces, and comments from JavaScript, CSS, and HTML files, making them smaller and faster to load. Minifying code enhances loading efficiency without altering the functionality, making it a powerful technique for improving site speed.

- **How to Minify Code**:
    - **Use Minification Tools**: Tools like UglifyJS for JavaScript, CSSNano for CSS, and HTMLMinifier for HTML can compress code quickly. These tools eliminate extraneous elements that slow down loading.
    - **CMS Plugins**: Content management systems like WordPress offer plugins, such as WP Rocket or Autoptimize, which can minify code automatically across your site, reducing file sizes and improving speed.
    - **Combine Files**: Combining multiple CSS or JavaScript files into single files can reduce the number of HTTP requests made by the browser, which speeds up page loading.

- **Best Practices**:
    - **Test After Minification**: Occasionally, minification can disrupt functionality, so always test your site after minifying code to ensure it loads and performs as expected.
    - **Exclude Critical Files if Needed**: Certain JavaScript files required for user interaction may not benefit from minification. Exclude them if minification impacts performance negatively.

3. CDN Usage: Reducing Latency with Content Delivery Networks

A Content Delivery Network (CDN) is a network of servers distributed globally that delivers content to users based on their geographic location. CDNs store copies of your site's assets on multiple servers, allowing users to load content from a server close to them, reducing latency and improving load times for international audiences.

- **How to Implement a CDN**:
    - **Select a CDN Provider**: Providers like Cloudflare, Amazon CloudFront, and Akamai offer CDN services with different pricing and features. Choose one that aligns with your website's needs and traffic volume.
    - **Integrate with Your Site**: Many CDN providers offer easy integration with popular CMS platforms. For WordPress, plugins like Cloudflare CDN can connect your site to the CDN with minimal setup.
    - **Cache Static Content**: CDNs are most effective for caching static files such as images, CSS, and JavaScript. This reduces the load on your origin server and improves load times for users.

- **Best Practices**:
    - **Enable Caching**: Leverage the caching options provided by CDNs to store static assets, ensuring that frequently accessed content loads faster for users.
    - **Use CDN Analytics**: Many CDNs offer analytics to track performance, allowing you to monitor load speeds, server response times, and user locations for optimal performance.

Bringing It All Together: Optimizing Site Speed

Improving site speed through image compression, code minification, and CDN usage is essential for maintaining strong rankings and a positive user experience in an AI-optimized world. These techniques help deliver faster, more efficient page loads, aligning with search engines' emphasis on performance and Core Web Vitals. By integrating these speed optimization practices into your technical SEO strategy, you can reduce bounce rates, increase engagement, and ensure that your site meets the standards of AI-driven search algorithms, enhancing your competitiveness.

B. Mobile-First and Responsive Design Strategies

With the shift to mobile-first indexing, search engines prioritize websites that provide a seamless experience on mobile devices. This change, driven by AI and user behavior, makes mobile optimization a critical aspect of technical SEO. Mobile-first and responsive design strategies ensure that websites are accessible, fast, and visually appealing on all devices, especially smartphones. Techniques such as AMP pages and responsive frameworks improve user experience, decrease bounce rates, and enhance search engine rankings, helping websites meet the needs of an increasingly mobile-driven audience. Here's how to implement mobile-first and responsive design strategies to stay competitive.

1. AMP Pages: Accelerating Mobile Load Times

Accelerated Mobile Pages (AMP) are a Google-backed initiative designed to improve mobile page load speeds by using streamlined HTML, limited JavaScript, and optimized caching. AMP pages load significantly faster than standard mobile pages, providing a smooth and efficient experience for users. AMP is especially beneficial for content-heavy sites, news articles, and e-commerce pages, where fast load times directly impact engagement and conversions.

- **How to Implement AMP**:
    - **Use AMP HTML**: AMP requires a simplified HTML structure. Google provides a framework for AMP-specific HTML, CSS, and JavaScript to reduce page load times while maintaining essential functions.
    - **CMS Integration and Plugins**: Many CMS platforms, like WordPress, offer AMP plugins that automatically convert pages to AMP-compatible formats. The official AMP plugin for WordPress simplifies setup and offers customization options.
    - **Verify with Google's AMP Validator**: After creating AMP pages, use Google's AMP Validator to ensure compliance. This tool checks for errors that may impact the performance and functionality of AMP pages.

- **Best Practices**:
    - **Prioritize Critical Content**: Display the most important content first on AMP pages, ensuring users can access key information instantly.
    - **Track Performance with AMP Analytics**: AMP has built-in analytics that allows you to monitor user behavior, engagement, and load times, helping optimize the mobile experience continuously.

2. Responsive Frameworks: Adapting to Multiple Devices and Screen Sizes

Responsive frameworks ensure that your website automatically adjusts to fit different screen sizes and devices. Using CSS media queries and flexible grids, responsive design provides a seamless experience on desktops, tablets, and smartphones alike. Popular responsive frameworks, like Bootstrap and Foundation, offer pre-built grid systems and components that simplify the design and development process, ensuring your site looks polished and performs well on any device.

- **How to Implement Responsive Design with Frameworks**:
    - **Use a Framework Like Bootstrap**: Bootstrap provides a grid system, responsive components, and utilities for designing layouts that adapt to screen sizes. It allows you to define column structures and use breakpoints to optimize content for various devices.
    - **Set Up Media Queries**: Media queries in CSS enable you to specify styles for different device types and screen resolutions. By setting breakpoints, you can adjust font sizes, image dimensions, and layout features to match mobile, tablet, and desktop views.
    - **Optimize for Touch Interactions**: Design elements like buttons and links to be touch-friendly, with adequate spacing and easily tappable areas. This improves usability on mobile devices and enhances experience.

- **Best Practices**:
    - **Prioritize Content Hierarchy for Mobile Users**: Display the most critical information at the top of the page, as mobile users typically scroll less. Simplify navigation and keep content concise to improve readability on smaller screens.
    - **Optimize Images and Multimedia for**

Responsive Layouts: Use flexible images and avoid fixed dimensions. Implement responsive image techniques like srcset to load appropriately sized images based on screen resolution and device type.

Mobile-First Design Principles: Designing for Mobile Users First

With mobile-first indexing, search engines primarily evaluate the mobile version of a website for indexing and ranking. Mobile-first design involves prioritizing mobile usability from the start, rather than designing for desktop and adapting for mobile afterward. By focusing on mobile-first principles, businesses can ensure their sites meet the needs of mobile users and align with search engines' criteria.

- **How to Apply Mobile-First Design**:
    - **Start with Mobile Layouts**: Begin by designing pages for mobile devices, focusing on simplicity and essential content. Consider how elements will appear on a small screen, and avoid clutter.
    - **Optimize Fonts and Buttons for Mobile**: Ensure text is legible on smaller screens by using larger fonts and sufficient line spacing. Buttons and CTAs should be sized for easy tapping, reducing the chance of accidental clicks.
    - **Test Across Devices**: Use tools like Google's Mobile-Friendly Test and BrowserStack to preview how your site appears on different devices and browsers. Testing helps identify usability issues that may not be apparent on desktop.

- **Best Practices**:

- **Limit Pop-Ups and Interstitials**: Mobile users often find pop-ups disruptive. Keep interstitials to a minimum, as excessive pop-ups can negatively impact user experience and, consequently, rankings.
- **Ensure Consistency Between Mobile and Desktop Content**: Google's mobile-first indexing favors sites where the mobile version matches the desktop version. Ensure that essential content, metadata, and structured data are consistent across all versions of the site.

Bringing It All Together: Building a Mobile-Optimized, Responsive Site for AI-Driven Search

Adopting AMP, responsive frameworks, and mobile-first principles are essential strategies for ensuring your site performs well across all devices in an AI-optimized environment. By focusing on fast load times, adaptable layouts, and user-friendly mobile experiences, you can improve search rankings, enhance user engagement, and meet the expectations of today's mobile-first users. With a responsive, mobile-first design strategy in place, your site will be better positioned to thrive, providing a seamless experience that aligns with search engines' evolving priorities.

C. Ensuring Website Security and Trust

Website security and user trust have become critical components of technical SEO, especially as search engines and AI-driven algorithms increasingly prioritize secure and trustworthy sites. Ensuring that your site is secure not only protects user data but also improves search rankings and builds credibility with visitors.

Implementing SSL certificates and maintaining clear privacy policies are essential steps in establishing a secure and transparent online presence. Here's how to enhance website security and trust through these vital strategies.

1. SSL Certificates: Encrypting Data and Boosting SEO

SSL (Secure Sockets Layer) certificates provide encryption for data transmitted between users and your website, ensuring that sensitive information, such as personal details and payment information, remains secure. Websites with SSL certificates have URLs that start with "https://" rather than "http://," and many browsers display a padlock icon to indicate that the site is secure. SSL not only protects user data but is also a ranking factor for search engines, meaning that sites without SSL may experience lower rankings.

- **How to Implement SSL Certificates**:
    - **Choose an SSL Certificate Type**: Select the right SSL certificate based on your needs. Options include Domain Validation (DV) for basic security, Organization Validation (OV) for business verification, and Extended Validation (EV) for maximum credibility with a green address bar.
    - **Obtain and Install the Certificate**: SSL certificates can be purchased through your web hosting provider or SSL vendors like Comodo or DigiCert. Once acquired, the certificate must be installed on your web server, which your hosting provider can often assist with.
    - **Update Internal Links**: After installing SSL, update internal links to use HTTPS instead of HTTP to avoid mixed content warnings. Use tools like a search-and-replace plugin or your CMS settings to ensure all links are secure.

- **Best Practices**:
  - **Redirect HTTP to HTTPS**: Use a 301 redirect to ensure that users are automatically directed to the HTTPS version of your site. This prevents duplicate content issues and helps consolidate traffic to the secure version.
  - **Monitor SSL Certificate Expiration**: SSL certificates have expiration dates and need to be renewed periodically. Set reminders to renew your certificate to avoid lapses in security, which can lead to warning messages for users and potential ranking drops.

2. Privacy Policies: Building Transparency and Compliance

A well-documented privacy policy is essential for gaining user trust and meeting legal requirements, especially with the rise of data protection regulations such as GDPR (General Data Protection Regulation) in the EU and CCPA (California Consumer Privacy Act) in the United States. Privacy policies inform users about the data you collect, how it's used, and their rights, making it easier for users to feel secure when visiting your site.

- **How to Create a Privacy Policy**:
  - **Outline Data Collection Practices**: Clearly state what types of data are collected (e.g., cookies, IP addresses, email addresses) and explain why you collect this information. Detail any third-party tools or services that have access to user data, such as Google Analytics or ad networks.
  - **Explain Data Usage and Sharing**: Describe how collected data is used, whether for personalization, analytics, or marketing, and

clarify under what circumstances data might be shared with third parties.
- **Include User Rights**: Inform users of their rights, such as the right to access, correct, or delete their data. For GDPR compliance, state how users can opt out of data tracking and request data deletion.

- **Best Practices**:
  - **Keep the Language Clear and Simple**: Avoid legal jargon to make your privacy policy accessible to all users. Straightforward language improves transparency and trust.
  - **Link to the Privacy Policy on Every Page**: Place a link to your privacy policy in the footer of your site, ensuring it's easily accessible from any page. This demonstrates openness and compliance with regulatory guidelines.
  - **Update Regularly for Compliance**: As data protection laws evolve, review and update your privacy policy to maintain compliance. This practice protects your business and shows users that you prioritize their privacy.

3. Additional Security Measures to Improve Trust

Beyond SSL and privacy policies, implementing additional security practices can further protect your site and build trust with users. These measures reduce the risk of data breaches, increase user confidence, and contribute to a positive reputation for your website.

- **Use a Web Application Firewall (WAF)**: A WAF monitors and filters traffic to protect against threats like SQL injections and DDoS attacks. Many hosting providers offer WAF solutions, which add an extra layer of security to your website.

- **Enable Two-Factor Authentication (2FA)**: Requiring two-factor authentication for user and admin logins adds an additional security layer, helping to prevent unauthorized access.

- **Regularly Back Up Your Site**: Scheduled backups protect your site's data and make it easier to recover from potential breaches. Many CMS platforms and hosting providers offer automated backup options, ensuring your data is safe.

Bringing It All Together: Securing Your Site to Meet AI-Driven SEO Standards

Ensuring website security through SSL certificates, privacy policies, and additional safeguards builds user trust, meets regulatory standards, and aligns with search engines' emphasis on secure and credible sites. By prioritizing data protection and transparency, you can improve rankings, protect user information, and foster confidence in your site, helping you thrive in where security and trust are valued.

D. Advanced Crawling and Indexing Strategies

As search engines become more sophisticated, managing how your website is crawled and indexed has become a crucial component of technical SEO. Efficiently utilizing your crawl budget and properly handling dynamic content ensures that search engines can access and index your most valuable pages, improving visibility and performance in search results. By implementing advanced crawling and indexing strategies, you can help search engines better understand your content, prioritize important pages, and maintain a high level of site efficiency. Here's how to optimize crawl budget and handle dynamic content to enhance your site's performance in AI-driven search engines.

1. Crawl Budget Optimization: Prioritizing Key Pages for Search Engines

Crawl budget refers to the number of pages a search engine crawls on your website within a given timeframe. Optimizing your crawl budget is essential for large or complex sites, as it ensures that search engines spend their resources on the most important and valuable pages, rather than wasting resources on low-priority or duplicate content.

- **How to Optimize Crawl Budget**:
    - **Use Robots.txt to Block Unnecessary Pages**: Use the robots.txt file to prevent search engines from crawling low-value pages, such as admin pages, login screens, and parameterized URLs. This helps focus the crawl budget on pages that contribute to search rankings.
    - **Set Up a Clear XML Sitemap**: An XML sitemap provides search engines with a roadmap of your site's important pages. Regularly update the sitemap and submit it to Google Search Console and Bing Webmaster Tools, ensuring that only essential pages are included.
    - **Consolidate Duplicate Content**: Use canonical tags to indicate the preferred version of a page when there are duplicates or near-duplicates. This allows search engines to focus on the canonical versions.

    - **Limit URL Parameters and Pagination**: Parameterized URLs and excessive pagination can create numerous variations of the same page, confusing search engines and consuming crawl budget. Use canonical tags, parameter settings in Google Search Console, or pagination controls to help search engines understand which URLs to prioritize.

- **Best Practices**:
    - **Monitor Crawl Stats in Google Search Console**: Regularly review the Crawl Stats report to see which pages are being crawled most frequently. Identify and address any low-priority pages that are consuming crawl budget unnecessarily.
    - **Ensure Fast Load Times**: Slow-loading pages can reduce the number of pages search engines can crawl. Improving site speed and optimizing Core Web Vitals helps search engines crawl more efficiently.

2. Handling Dynamic Content: Ensuring Visibility for AJAX, JavaScript, and User-Generated Content

Dynamic content—such as JavaScript-based, AJAX, or user-generated content—can enhance user experience but may pose challenges for search engine crawling and indexing. Implementing strategies that make dynamic content accessible to search engines ensures that your most engaging elements are visible in search results.

- **How to Optimize Dynamic Content for Crawling and Indexing**:
    - **Server-Side Rendering (SSR) for JavaScript**: Search engines often struggle to crawl client-side JavaScript, which is rendered on the user's browser rather than on the server. Use server-side rendering (SSR) or dynamic rendering to ensure that JavaScript content is fully rendered

before it reaches the search engine, making it easier to crawl.
- **Use Lazy Loading Carefully**: Lazy loading defers the loading of certain elements (e.g., images) until they're in view, improving page speed. However, improper lazy loading can prevent search engines from seeing all content. Ensure that important images and content are still accessible and avoid lazy loading critical text content.
- **Progressive Enhancement for AJAX**: AJAX loads content dynamically without refreshing the page, but this can hide content from search engines if not implemented carefully. Use progressive enhancement to ensure that all critical content loads statically for search engines while enhancing it with AJAX for users.
- **Use "Fetch as Google" in Search Console**: Google's Fetch tool allows you to see how Googlebot renders your dynamic pages. This helps identify any parts of your site that are not being indexed due to rendering issues, allowing you to address these problems directly.

- **Best Practices**:
  - **Create Static Versions for High-Value Dynamic Pages**: If specific dynamic content is vital for SEO, consider creating a static version of these pages, especially for important landing pages or product pages. This ensures that search engines can easily access and index critical information.
  - **Review the Mobile Version for Dynamic Content**: Since Google uses mobile-first indexing, ensure that all dynamic content loads properly on mobile devices. Test dynamic elements on mobile to verify that they're visible to both users and search engines.

3. Structured Data to Aid Crawling and Indexing

Structured data provides additional context for search engines, helping them understand and categorize your content more efficiently. Marking up your site with structured data (using schema markup) can improve how search engines process complex content, enhancing both crawling efficiency and indexing accuracy.

- **How to Implement Structured Data for Improved Indexing**:
    - **Apply Schema Markup to Key Pages**: Use structured data on high-priority pages to help search engines understand content types, such as articles, products, FAQs, and reviews. Schema markup allows search engines to recognize the purpose and relevance of these pages quickly.
    - **Add Breadcrumbs for Navigation Structure**: Breadcrumb schema markup enhances internal linking and shows search engines how your site's hierarchy is organized. Breadcrumbs also provide additional context for users, improving usability and indexing efficiency.
    - **Monitor Structured Data in Search Console**: Use the "Enhancements" report in Google Search Console to monitor errors and warnings in your structured data, addressing any issues that could affect how pages are indexed.

Bringing It All Together: Optimizing Crawling and Indexing for AI-Driven Search Engines

Efficiently managing your crawl budget and making

dynamic content accessible to search engines are essential strategies for improving visibility in AI-driven search engines. By focusing on the most important pages, ensuring dynamic content is crawlable, and adding structured data, you create a more efficient and optimized site that AI algorithms can easily interpret. These advanced crawling and indexing strategies not only improve SEO performance but also help your site maintain a competitive edge.

Chapter 12. Voice Search and Natural Language Optimization

With the rise of voice-activated devices like Amazon Alexa, Google Assistant, and Apple's Siri, optimizing for voice search has become an essential part of modern SEO. Voice search differs significantly from traditional text-based searches, as users tend to speak in full sentences and natural language rather than typing keywords. This shift requires businesses to adapt their content to be conversational, concise, and highly relevant to common questions and intents. Natural language optimization enhances a site's ability to capture voice search traffic by aligning with how people naturally speak and ask questions. Here's how to optimize for voice search and natural language.

A. Understanding Voice Search Behavior

As voice-activated technology becomes more integrated into daily life, understanding the behavior of voice search users is essential for optimizing content effectively. Voice search users tend to have distinct habits, including specific demographics, query patterns, and intents that differ from traditional search. Tailoring content to these behaviors can improve visibility in voice search results and ensure your content aligns with user expectations. Here's an overview of the primary demographics, types of queries, and intents that characterize voice search behavior.

1. User Demographics: Who Uses Voice Search?

Voice search is popular across a wide range of

demographics, but certain groups show particularly high adoption rates. Understanding the demographics of voice search users can help you better target your content and align it with the needs and preferences of your audience.

- **Key Demographic Trends**:
  - **Younger Users**: Studies show that younger audiences, particularly those in the 18-34 age range, are the most frequent users of voice search. They tend to be early adopters of technology and favor the convenience of voice assistants like Siri, Alexa, and Google Assistant.
  - **Mobile and On-the-Go Users**: Voice search is often used on mobile devices, particularly by users on the go. Mobile voice search is common in situations where typing isn't convenient, such as driving or multitasking.
  - **Smart Home Device Owners**: The popularity of smart home devices (e.g., Amazon Echo, Google Nest) has also fueled voice search usage. These users are accustomed to interacting with voice-activated devices for a range of tasks, from retrieving information to controlling smart home functions.

- **Best Practices**:
  - **Optimize for Mobile and Local Search**: Since many voice search users are mobile and looking for quick answers, focus on mobile optimization and local SEO to meet the needs of users who seek local information or directions.
  - **Consider Younger Audiences in Content Tone**: Use a friendly, conversational tone in your content, which aligns well with the preferences of younger, tech-savvy users who often use voice search.

2. Common Queries: Types and Patterns of Voice Search Questions

Voice search queries are often longer, more conversational, and context-specific compared to text-based searches. Users tend to ask full questions rather than using short keywords, making it important to structure content that addresses these query patterns effectively.

- **Types of Common Queries in Voice Search**:
    - **Question-Based Queries**: Voice search users frequently use question words like "how," "what," "where," "when," and "why." Examples include "How do I start a vegetable garden?" or "What's the best way to make coffee?" Structuring content to answer these questions directly can improve your chances of appearing in voice search results.
    - **Local and "Near Me" Searches**: Many voice search users look for local businesses or services, often with phrases like "near me." Examples include "Find a bookstore near me" or "Where's the closest ATM?" Optimizing for local SEO and including location-based keywords can capture these types of queries.
    - **Intent-Based Queries**: Users often have a clear intent when using voice search, such as finding a product, researching a topic, or getting step-by-step instructions. Queries like "Buy eco-friendly shampoo" or "Directions to the nearest gas station" indicate a need for immediate, actionable information.

- **Best Practices**:
    - **Target Long-Tail and Conversational Keywords**: Voice search queries are typically longer and more detailed. Focusing on long-tail

keywords that match natural speech patterns, such as "best running shoes for beginners," increases the likelihood of capturing voice traffic.
  - **Address Specific User Intent**: Identify the types of intents common among your audience (e.g., informational, navigational, transactional) and tailor content to meet these needs. For instance, create how-to guides for informational queries and clear product pages for transactional queries.

Bringing It All Together: Tailoring Content to Voice Search Behavior

Understanding the demographics and behavior patterns of voice search users is essential for creating optimized content. By focusing on the younger, mobile-first audience that frequently uses voice search, targeting question-based and local queries, and aligning content with user intent, you can increase your visibility and relevance in voice search results. In the next sections, we'll dive deeper into strategies for structuring content for quick answers, optimizing for natural language, and leveraging FAQs to further enhance your site's voice search readiness.

B. Optimizing for Conversational Queries

With the rise of voice search, optimizing for conversational queries has become essential. Unlike traditional typed searches, voice search queries are more natural, often involving complete sentences or questions. Users tend to phrase their searches conversationally, asking questions that reflect how they speak in real life. To capture this traffic, businesses must focus on long-tail keywords, question-based content, and natural language optimization.

Here's how to tailor your content for conversational queries, improving your chances of ranking for voice searches.

1. Targeting Long-Tail Keywords for Conversational Search

Long-tail keywords are phrases that are more specific and detailed, often containing three or more words. These keywords closely match how people naturally phrase their questions in voice searches and are essential for capturing intent-driven traffic. Long-tail keywords not only align with voice search patterns but also tend to have lower competition, making it easier to rank for highly specific queries.

- **How to Identify Long-Tail Keywords**:
    - **Use Voice Search-Specific Keyword Tools**: Tools like Answer the Public, SEMrush's Keyword Magic Tool, and Google's "People Also Ask" feature can provide insights into long-tail keywords and popular question phrases in your industry.
    - **Focus on Intent-Based Phrases**: Consider the intent behind a user's search. For example, instead of targeting "running shoes," focus on long-tail phrases like "best running shoes for beginners" or "affordable running shoes with arch support."
    - **Incorporate Local Modifiers**: If you cater to a local audience, include location-specific keywords (e.g., "best vegan restaurants in Seattle") to capture local voice search traffic.

- **Best Practices**:
    - **Write Naturally**: Avoid "stuffing" keywords into your content. Use long-tail keywords naturally within sentences to match how people would

speak in real life.
- **Use Subheadings for Different Queries**: Break up content with subheadings that contain long-tail keywords, improving readability and helping search engines identify relevant sections.

2. Creating Question-Based Content for Voice Search

Question-based content mirrors how users phrase their searches when using voice-activated devices. Structuring your content to answer common questions directly can improve your chances of appearing in voice search results, particularly in response to informational queries that seek quick answers.

- **How to Structure Question-Based Content**:
    - **Add FAQ Sections**: Create FAQ sections that address common questions within your industry or related to your products. Each question should be phrased exactly as users might say it, such as "How do I make cold brew coffee at home?" followed by a straightforward answer.
    - **Use Header Tags (H2 and H3) for Questions**: Format each question as a header (H2 or H3) to help search engines identify question-answer pairs. This structure makes it easier for search engines to display your content as a featured snippet, which is commonly used in voice search results.
    - **Answer in Concise, Direct Language**: Provide clear, concise answers directly below each question. Aim to answer the question in the first sentence or two, followed by more detailed information if necessary. This structure helps voice search algorithms identify the main answer quickly.

- **Best Practices**:
  - **Include Common "How," "What," and "Why" Questions**: Use a mix of question types, as voice search queries often start with words like "how," "what," and "why." For example, "What are the benefits of yoga?" or "How do I install a water filter?"
  - **Create "How-To" and Tutorial Content**: For informational queries, create step-by-step guides or "how-to" articles that respond to questions users frequently ask. Structured content like this is valuable for voice search users seeking quick instructions.

3. Using Conversational Language to Improve Readability and Relatability

Voice search algorithms favor content that reads naturally, reflecting how people speak in everyday conversation. Adopting a conversational tone makes your content more accessible and relatable, increasing the likelihood that it will be chosen by AI-driven voice assistants.

- **How to Use Conversational Language**:
  - **Write as if You're Speaking to the Reader**: Use a friendly and approachable tone, avoiding overly formal or complex language. For example, instead of saying "Optimal hydration techniques," use simpler phrases like "ways to stay hydrated."
  - **Break Up Content with Simple Sentences**: Use short sentences and avoid jargon, making content easy to understand for a broad audience. The simpler the language, the more accessible it will be for voice search.
  - **Include Transitional Phrases**: Words like "first," "next," and "finally" can guide readers

through steps and make content easier to follow, which is especially helpful for "how-to" and instructional queries.

- **Best Practices**:
  - **Anticipate Follow-Up Questions**: Think about what additional questions users might have and address them in your content. For example, if you answer "How do I grow basil indoors?" also cover questions like "What's the best light for growing basil?" or "How often should I water basil indoors?"
  - **Use Personal Pronouns and Direct Language**: Address the reader directly with "you" to make the content feel more engaging and relevant.

Bringing It All Together: Crafting Content for Conversational Queries in Voice Search

Optimizing for conversational queries in voice search involves using long-tail keywords, structuring content around common questions, and adopting a natural, conversational tone. By tailoring your content to match how people speak and ask questions, you increase the chances of appearing in voice search results and improving engagement.

C. Structuring Content for Featured Snippets

Featured snippets are highly visible search results that appear at the top of Google's SERPs, offering concise answers to user queries. Structuring your content to target featured snippets is essential for optimizing for voice search, as AI assistants frequently pull responses from these snippets. To increase your chances of earning a featured snippet, organize your content in ways that allow search engines to quickly identify and extract relevant information. Here's how to structure content using paragraphs, lists, and tables to maximize the likelihood of capturing featured snippets.

1. Paragraph Snippets: Providing Concise, Direct Answers

Paragraph snippets typically provide a brief, 40-60 word response to a question, delivering a quick answer directly within the search results. These snippets are often used for definitions, summaries, or direct answers to questions like "What is SEO?" or "How does photosynthesis work?"

- **How to Structure for Paragraph Snippets:**
    - **Answer the Question in the First Sentence**: Start with a concise answer to the query. For example, for a question like "What is content marketing?" begin with a direct answer, such as "Content marketing is a strategy focused on creating and sharing valuable content to attract and retain a target audience."
    - **Expand Briefly with Additional Information**: After the initial answer, provide one or two more sentences to add context or detail. This approach helps satisfy users who want a quick answer while giving enough information to engage those who may read further.
    - **Use Header Tags for Clear Organization**: Place the question as an H2 or H3 header above the paragraph. This structure signals to search engines that the text below directly answers the query.

- **Best Practices**:
  - **Keep It Brief and Relevant**: Aim for 40-60 words in your response, as Google typically prefers short, direct answers in paragraph snippets.
  - **Use Natural Language**: Write in a conversational and clear style that aligns with how people ask questions. Avoid jargon and complex phrasing to improve readability.

2. List Snippets: Providing Step-by-Step or Enumerated Information

List snippets are commonly used for "how-to" queries, rankings, comparisons, or lists of tips and benefits. Google often displays list snippets as numbered or bulleted lists, making them ideal for step-by-step guides or top lists (e.g., "Best productivity tips" or "Steps to apply for a passport").

- **How to Structure for List Snippets**:
  - **Use Clear Subheadings or Numbered Steps**: For step-by-step guides, use numbered steps or bullet points to break down the information. For example, if creating a "How to bake a cake" guide, list each step in order, such as "1. Preheat the oven to 350°F" and "2. Mix the ingredients."
  - **Keep Each Point Brief**: Make each bullet point or numbered item concise, ideally one sentence. This makes it easier for search engines to pull individual steps or tips as a list.
  - **Use Ordered or Unordered Lists**: Format the list as either ordered (numbered) for sequential instructions or unordered (bulleted) for non-sequential lists. This choice helps Google display the list in the intended format.

- **Best Practices**:
    - **Address the Query in the Header**: Start with a header that clearly states the query, such as "How to Create a Marketing Plan." Follow this with the list, as it increases the likelihood of Google selecting the entire section as a featured snippet.
    - **Use Simple, Action-Oriented Language**: Write each item in a clear, actionable way to improve readability and user comprehension.

3. Table Snippets: Organizing Data for Comparisons and Statistics

Table snippets are effective for content that involves comparisons, data summaries, or statistics, such as product comparisons, pricing details, or survey results. Google extracts these tables to display structured data that allows users to view information at a glance.

- **How to Structure for Table Snippets**:
    - **Create Simple, Well-Organized Tables**: Use HTML tables or table options within your CMS to format the data. Keep tables simple, with clear headers for each column and row to make the information easy to read and understand.
    - **Label Columns Clearly**: Label each column and row concisely, using terms that directly relate to the query. For example, a table comparing smartphones could have columns labeled "Model," "Battery Life," "Camera Quality," and "Price."
    - **Limit the Number of Rows and Columns**: Google tends to favor smaller tables that display essential information concisely. Try to keep tables under 5-6 rows and 3-4 columns for easy readability in featured snippets.

- **Best Practices**:
  - **Use Descriptive Headers**: Add a descriptive header above the table, such as "Comparison of Top Smartphones 2024." This helps search engines recognize the table's purpose and relevance to user queries.
  - **Present Key Data Only**: Include only the most relevant data points to avoid overwhelming users with too much information. Summarizing key details improves the table's chances of being selected for a snippet.

Bringing It All Together: Structuring Content to Capture Featured Snippets

By structuring content as paragraphs, lists, and tables, you make it easier for search engines to extract relevant answers and present them as featured snippets. Use direct answers in paragraphs, organize step-by-step processes in lists, and summarize data in tables to align with common snippet formats. Optimizing for featured snippets not only boosts visibility but also improves your content's appeal for voice search, as AI assistants frequently pull answers from snippet-friendly content. This structured approach helps you maximize your chances of ranking prominently in search results, meeting both user needs and AI-driven preferences.

D. Utilizing Voice Schema Markup

With the growing popularity of voice search, schema markup specifically designed for voice-activated devices can enhance your content's chances of being read aloud by virtual assistants like Google Assistant and Amazon Alexa. *Speakable* schema markup, for example, is particularly beneficial for news and article content, as it highlights sections of text that are suitable for audio playback. By implementing *Speakable* schema, you can optimize your site's content for voice-driven interactions, making it more accessible for users who rely on voice search and helping boost your content's visibility on AI-driven platforms. Here's how to use *Speakable* schema effectively for voice search optimization.

1. Understanding *Speakable* Schema: Optimizing for Audio Content Delivery

Speakable schema markup is designed to identify sections of content suitable for audio playback by voice-activated devices. This type of schema is especially useful for news articles, blog posts, and other content with clearly defined summaries or key takeaways. By using *Speakable* schema, you can guide AI assistants to read specific sections aloud, giving your content more exposure in voice search results.

- **How *Speakable* Schema Works**:
    - **Highlights Key Points**: *Speakable* schema lets you mark up key phrases, summaries, or highlights of an article. This allows virtual assistants to identify the most important parts of the content and deliver them as a quick, spoken summary to users.
    - **Enhances Voice Search Relevance**: By focusing on specific, digestible phrases, *Speakable* schema ensures that virtual assistants can quickly and accurately deliver relevant information to users, enhancing the content's usability in voice search.

- **Ideal Use Cases**:
    - **News Articles and Breaking News**: Short

news articles that provide concise, relevant information are ideal for *Speakable* schema. Marking up the introductory paragraph or the key takeaways of a news article can make it easier for AI to read them aloud.
  - **Summaries and Lists in Articles**: For blog posts or articles, using *Speakable* schema on summaries or list items (such as "top tips" or "key points") makes it easier for voice assistants to present key information to users.

2. How to Implement *Speakable* Schema for News and Articles

To implement *Speakable* schema, you need to add structured data to your webpage, marking up the specific parts of the content you want to make available for audio playback. This can be done with JSON-LD, which is the preferred format for structured data.

- **Steps to Implement *Speakable* Schema**:
  - **Identify Key Content for Voice Playback**: Choose sections that provide clear, concise summaries or important points from the article. Aim for 20-30 words per marked section to keep it concise and easy for AI to read aloud.

Use JSON-LD to Add *Speakable* Markup: Insert *Speakable* schema using JSON-LD format within your HTML.

For example:

```
{
  "@context": "https://schema.org",
  "@type": "NewsArticle",
  "headline": "Example Headline for Article",
  "speakable": {
    "@type": "SpeakableSpecification",
    "xpath": [
      "/html/body/div[1]/article/section[1]/p[1]",
      "/html/body/div[1]/article/section[1]/p[2]"
    ]
  }
}
```

- In this example, the *Speakable* schema marks specific paragraphs within the article for audio playback. Adjust the XPath to match the structure of your HTML and ensure that it highlights the intended content sections.
- **Verify with Google's Rich Results Test**: After adding the schema, use Google's Rich Results Test tool to validate the markup. This tool helps identify any errors and confirm that *Speakable* schema is properly implemented for your content.

- **Best Practices**:
    - **Prioritize Clarity and Brevity**: Choose content that conveys the main points quickly. AI assistants prioritize clear, succinct text that users can absorb easily in an audio format.
    - **Use Natural, Conversational Language**: The highlighted text should be written in a conversational tone, making it easier to listen to when read aloud by voice assistants.

3. Other Types of Voice-Friendly Schema for Enhanced Engagement

In addition to *Speakable* schema, consider using other structured data types that improve voice search visibility, such as FAQ, How-To, and Q&A schema. These formats help organize content in ways that align well with voice search behavior, making it easier for AI to understand and present your content to users.

- **FAQ and Q&A Schema**: Marking up frequently asked questions allows voice assistants to identify and directly answer common user queries.

- **How-To Schema**: For instructional content, How-To schema can break down steps in a format that's easy for voice search to read aloud, enhancing usability for DIY and instructional queries.

Bringing It All Together: Enhancing Content for Voice Search with *Speakable* Schema

Utilizing *Speakable* schema markup for news articles and key article takeaways can significantly increase your content's relevance in voice search. By highlighting specific, concise portions of text that lend themselves to audio playback, you improve the accessibility and engagement potential of your content on AI-driven platforms. Integrating *Speakable* and other voice-friendly schema markups into your content strategy ensures that your site remains competitive in voice search, making your information easily accessible to a growing audience.

Chapter 13. AI-Powered Tools for SEO and Marketing

AI-powered tools have become indispensable for SEO and marketing professionals. These tools streamline complex tasks, provide deep insights, and automate processes that once required extensive time and expertise. From predictive analytics and keyword optimization to content generation and personalization, AI tools enable marketers to work smarter, enhance accuracy, and respond quickly to market shifts.

A. SEO Automation Tools

SEO automation tools powered by AI have become essential for streamlining tasks that require precision, consistency, and frequent updates. These tools allow marketers to automate core functions like keyword research and rank tracking, helping them stay agile. By leveraging automation, SEO professionals can focus more on strategy and creative problem-solving while staying on top of the latest trends and performance metrics. Here's how AI-powered tools are transforming keyword research and rank tracking for better, faster, and more accurate results.

1. Keyword Research Automation: Uncovering High-Value Opportunities

Keyword research is the foundation of any SEO strategy, but traditional methods can be time-consuming. AI-powered tools for keyword research help automate the process by analyzing vast amounts of data, uncovering high-value keywords, and providing insights into search intent. These tools quickly identify relevant keywords, search volumes, competition levels, and user trends, allowing marketers to target keywords that align with audience needs and drive traffic.

- **Top Tools for Automated Keyword Research**:
    - **SEMrush and Ahrefs**: These tools use AI to generate extensive lists of keywords, along with detailed metrics on search volume, keyword difficulty, and competitive analysis. They also offer related keyword suggestions, enabling marketers to discover long-tail and high-value keywords that match user intent.
    - **Surfer SEO**: By analyzing top-ranking pages, Surfer SEO provides keyword recommendations based on what's currently effective in search results. It also suggests semantic keywords and keyword clusters to help optimize content holistically.
    - **Answer The Public**: This tool provides insights into common questions users ask around a particular topic, helping marketers target question-based keywords that align with voice search and

user intent.

- **Best Practices for Using Automated Keyword Research**:
    - **Focus on Intent**: Use AI tools to identify keywords that match user intent, whether informational, transactional, or navigational. This helps create content that resonates with searchers and improves relevance in search engine rankings.
    - **Target Long-Tail and Low-Competition Keywords**: AI tools make it easier to identify long-tail keywords with lower competition, which can bring in highly targeted traffic and improve visibility for niche topics.

2. Rank Tracking Automation: Monitoring Performance and Adjusting Strategy

Rank tracking is essential for understanding how well your keywords are performing and identifying opportunities for improvement. AI-powered rank tracking tools automate this process, allowing marketers to monitor keyword performance across various search engines, track competitors' rankings, and receive alerts about significant changes. Automated rank tracking provides a clear picture of SEO progress, enabling marketers to make informed decisions without manually checking rankings.

- **Top Tools for Automated Rank Tracking**:
    - **Google Search Console**: As a free tool, Google Search Console provides detailed insights into keyword rankings, click-through rates, and visibility, helping track performance directly from the source.
    - **SERPWatcher by Mangools**: This tool monitors keyword positions, ranking trends, and estimated traffic potential, offering daily updates and visual tracking over time. It also provides insights into SERP volatility, helping identify when algorithm changes may be affecting rankings.
    - **Rank Ranger**: With customizable reports and advanced rank tracking, Rank Ranger enables marketers to monitor keyword rankings for different search engines and locations. It also provides white-label reports, useful for agencies working with clients.

- **Best Practices for Using Automated Rank Tracking**:
    - **Set Alerts for Significant Rank Changes**: Many rank-tracking tools allow users to set up alerts for major ranking shifts. This helps SEO professionals respond quickly to both improvements and declines.
    - **Monitor Competitor Performance**: Use rank-tracking tools to keep an eye on competitors' rankings for similar keywords, giving insights into where your

content may need adjustments to stay competitive.
- **Track Local and Mobile Rankings Separately**: Since search results vary based on location and device, monitor both local and mobile rankings to get a full picture of performance across user environments.

Bringing It All Together: Optimizing SEO with Automation Tools

Automated keyword research and rank tracking tools save time, reduce manual errors, and provide deeper insights into SEO performance. By integrating these tools into your SEO strategy, you can efficiently identify valuable keyword opportunities, monitor rankings consistently, and adjust your approach based on real-time data. Leveraging SEO automation tools empowers marketers to stay ahead, making smarter, data-driven decisions that improve rankings, drive traffic, and maximize engagement.

B. Content Creation and Curation Tools

AI-powered content creation and curation tools have revolutionized the way marketers develop, organize, and distribute content. From generating high-quality articles to curating relevant industry news, these tools help streamline content workflows, increase productivity, and ensure that audiences receive valuable, engaging information. AI-generated content tools enable rapid creation of SEO-optimized text, while content curation platforms make it easy to discover and share the latest industry trends. Here's how to effectively use AI-generated content and curation platforms to enhance your content strategy and keep your audience engaged.

1. AI-Generated Content: Enhancing Productivity and Creativity

AI-generated content tools use natural language processing (NLP) and machine learning algorithms to generate written content based on prompts, keywords, or specific guidelines. While these tools don't fully replace human creativity, they provide a foundation for blog posts, social media updates, product descriptions, and more. AI content generators are especially useful for scaling content production, saving time on drafting, and sparking new ideas.

- **Top Tools for AI-Generated Content**:
    - **Jasper**: Jasper (formerly known as Jarvis) is a popular AI writing assistant that produces articles, blog posts, social media content, and more. It offers templates for various content types and uses NLP to create natural-sounding text that aligns with user intent.
    - **ChatGPT**: As a conversational AI tool,

ChatGPT can generate responses, ideas, and content based on specific prompts. It is highly adaptable for creating informational content, answering user queries, and drafting outlines.
- **Copy.ai**: Copy.ai specializes in creating marketing copy, including headlines, social media posts, and short-form content. It's ideal for generating attention-grabbing text that resonates with audiences.

- **Best Practices for Using AI-Generated Content**:
    - **Use AI as a Starting Point**: AI-generated content can provide a quick draft or outline, but always review and refine the text to add your brand's unique voice.
    - **Optimize for SEO**: AI content tools often allow for keyword integration. Ensure that relevant keywords are included naturally, and check for proper structure to align with SEO best practices.
    - **Stay Authentic and Add Value**: AI tools can generate informative content, but it's essential to inject personal expertise and value. Use AI to handle repetitive or time-consuming tasks while focusing on adding unique, human insights.

2. Content Curation Platforms: Delivering Relevant, Engaging Information

Content curation platforms allow marketers to discover, organize, and share valuable content from other sources, positioning their brand as a thought leader in their industry. By curating relevant articles, news, and blog posts, businesses can offer audiences fresh perspectives, maintain consistent engagement, and keep content pipelines full without creating everything from scratch.

- **Top Tools for Content Curation**:
    - **Feedly**: Feedly aggregates content from various sources and uses AI to suggest relevant articles, news, and blog posts. It allows marketers to create topic-specific feeds, making it easy to find and share industry news that resonates with their audience.
    - **Pocket**: Pocket enables users to save articles, videos, and other content for later reading. It's useful for curating valuable resources that can be shared with audiences over time, especially through social media or email newsletters.
    - **BuzzSumo**: BuzzSumo identifies trending content, key influencers, and popular topics within specific industries. It's ideal for discovering high-engagement content that audiences find valuable, which can then be curated or serve as inspiration for original content.

- **Best Practices for Using Content Curation Platforms**:

- **Curate Content That Complements Your Brand**: Select content that aligns with your brand's values, audience interests, and goals. Adding brief commentary or summaries provides context and reinforces your expertise.
- **Balance Original and Curated Content**: Use curation as a supplement to your original content, maintaining a balance that keeps your brand voice strong while providing diverse insights.
- **Use Curation to Identify Trends and Topics**: Curated content reveals what's trending in your industry, helping you stay updated and identify potential topics for original content that will resonate with your audience.

3. Integrating Content Creation and Curation for a Comprehensive Strategy

Combining AI-generated content with curated material allows for a well-rounded content strategy that delivers both fresh perspectives and consistent engagement. AI tools can produce foundational content, while curation platforms ensure you're sharing relevant industry insights, establishing your brand as a trusted resource.

- **How to Integrate AI Content and Curation**:
  - **Use AI to Draft, Then Curate for Depth**: Use AI-generated content to create

foundational articles, then enrich them with curated insights or supporting data. For example, follow an AI-generated blog post with curated articles that add depth and reinforce key points.
- **Curate to Support Long-Form Content**: Curate industry news and trending articles to support white papers, ebooks, or blog series, keeping readers informed while connecting broader industry trends to your expertise.
- **Automate Social Sharing**: Use tools like Buffer or Hootsuite to schedule curated content alongside AI-generated social media posts, maintaining a consistent posting schedule across platforms.

Bringing It All Together: Enhancing Content Strategy with AI Creation and Curation

AI-generated content and curation platforms are powerful tools for maintaining an engaging and consistent content strategy. By using AI to streamline content creation and curation platforms to share valuable industry insights, you can save time, boost productivity, and establish authority in your niche. Together, these tools allow brands to stay current, reach broader audiences, and deliver high-quality content that aligns with both audience interests and SEO best practices.

C. Analytics and Data Interpretation

AI-powered analytics and data interpretation tools are essential for understanding user behavior and predicting future trends. By leveraging advanced analytics techniques like predictive analytics and user behavior modeling, businesses can make informed decisions, anticipate customer needs, and tailor their marketing strategies for maximum impact. These AI-powered tools allow marketers to gain deeper insights into audience preferences, identify emerging trends, and enhance user engagement, helping brands stay ahead in a competitive environment. Here's how to harness predictive analytics and user behavior modeling to interpret data and drive strategic growth.

1. Predictive Analytics: Anticipating Future Trends and Opportunities

Predictive analytics uses historical data, machine learning, and statistical algorithms to forecast future outcomes. For marketers, predictive analytics can help identify potential customer behaviors, trends, and revenue opportunities. By analyzing patterns, these tools make it possible to predict customer preferences, engagement likelihood, and even potential conversions, empowering businesses to make proactive and strategic decisions.

- **Top Tools for Predictive Analytics**:
    - **Google Analytics**: GA offers predictive metrics like purchase probability, churn

probability, and revenue prediction. These insights allow marketers to identify high-value customers, target retention efforts, and optimize ad spend.
- **Salesforce Einstein Analytics**: Salesforce's AI-driven analytics tool predicts customer behavior, sales trends, and opportunities. It integrates directly with customer relationship management (CRM) data, helping marketers personalize campaigns and improve customer engagement.
- **IBM Watson Analytics**: Known for its advanced AI capabilities, Watson Analytics helps interpret complex data sets and make predictions. It provides natural language processing (NLP)-based insights, making it easier to explore data and uncover actionable trends.

- **Best Practices for Using Predictive Analytics**:
    - **Set Clear Goals and Metrics**: Define specific outcomes you want to predict, such as customer retention or purchase probability, and set relevant KPIs. Clear goals help focus predictive efforts and measure success accurately.

    - **Use Predictive Insights to Segment Audiences**: Leverage predictions to create targeted segments, such as high-converting customers or users likely to churn. Tailor marketing efforts to each

segment based on predicted behavior.
- **Regularly Update and Validate Models**: Predictive models should be updated regularly to maintain accuracy. Validate predictions with real outcomes to improve and adjust models as needed.

2. User Behavior Modeling: Understanding and Anticipating User Actions

User behavior modeling analyzes data from user interactions, identifying patterns and trends that reveal how users engage with content, products, or services. These insights can inform content strategies, site layout, personalization efforts, and product recommendations. AI-powered user behavior models help marketers understand customer journeys, identify bottlenecks, and predict behaviors like abandonment, making it easier to create a user-centered experience that maximizes engagement and retention.

- **Top Tools for User Behavior Modeling**:
    - **Mixpanel**: Mixpanel focuses on tracking user actions and understanding the customer journey. It provides insights into user retention, feature adoption, and behavior trends, helping marketers optimize for each stage of the customer lifecycle.
    - **Hotjar**: Hotjar combines heatmaps, session recordings, and user feedback

to visualize user interactions. It helps marketers understand what drives engagement, where users drop off, and how to improve on-site experience.
- **Amplitude**: Amplitude provides advanced behavioral analytics that allow marketers to track user actions, build retention models, and analyze user paths. Its data-driven insights can help refine engagement and conversion strategies.

- **Best Practices for Using User Behavior Modeling**:
    - **Map Out Key User Journeys**: Define key actions users take (e.g., signing up, making a purchase, reading articles) and map out common journeys. User journey insights help identify areas where users may need additional support or encouragement to complete desired actions.
    - **Focus on Drop-Off Points**: Analyze where users drop off in the conversion funnel. Understanding where and why users leave can inform improvements that reduce bounce rates and increase engagement.
    - **Personalize Based on Behavioral Data**: Use behavioral insights to create personalized content or offers based on users' actions. For instance, suggest products based on past purchases or recommend content based on previous

page views.

3. Combining Predictive Analytics and User Behavior Modeling for Strategic Growth

When used together, predictive analytics and user behavior modeling provide a comprehensive view of current and future customer interactions. Predictive insights allow marketers to anticipate user actions and personalize campaigns, while behavior models reveal how users engage with content and products, offering opportunities for optimization.

- **How to Integrate Predictive Analytics and User Behavior Models**:
    - **Segment Users by Predicted Behavior**: Use predictive insights to segment users based on likely future actions, then apply behavior modeling to understand how they interact within each segment. For example, high-value users may have unique engagement patterns that can inform loyalty programs or exclusive offers.
    - **Develop Proactive Retention Strategies**: Predictive analytics can identify users at risk of churn, while user behavior models can reveal pain points in their journey. Together, these insights allow you to design proactive retention strategies, such as targeted offers or personalized follow-ups.

- **Refine Content and Product Recommendations**: By combining behavioral data with predictive models, marketers can refine product or content recommendations, tailoring suggestions to align with predicted user preferences and engagement patterns.

Bringing It All Together: Leveraging Analytics and AI for Data-Driven Growth

AI-powered analytics tools for predictive insights and user behavior modeling allow businesses to interpret complex data, anticipate user actions, and refine their strategies. By using predictive analytics to forecast trends and behavior modeling to understand engagement patterns, marketers can make data-driven decisions that improve user experience, increase retention, and maximize conversions. These AI-driven insights enable brands to act proactively, delivering personalized and meaningful interactions that foster loyalty and drive growth.

D. Chatbots and Virtual Assistants

Chatbots and virtual assistants powered by AI are transforming the way businesses engage with users on their websites. By providing immediate, interactive responses, these tools can enhance user experience, boost engagement, and increase conversion rates. Chatbots are especially effective for customer support, lead generation, and guiding users through the sales funnel, while virtual assistants offer a more advanced, conversational experience that can handle complex queries and personalize interactions. Here's how to use chatbots and virtual assistants to improve engagement on your site and build stronger customer relationships.

1. Benefits of Chatbots for User Engagement

Chatbots can handle a wide range of tasks, from answering frequently asked questions to assisting users with navigating your site. Available 24/7, chatbots offer real-time support, ensuring that users get the information they need without delay. This quick assistance keeps users engaged, reduces bounce rates, and can lead to higher conversion rates.

- **Key Benefits**:
    - **Immediate Responses**: Chatbots provide instant answers, improving user satisfaction and helping users resolve issues quickly without waiting for a human representative.
    - **Increased Engagement**: Interactive chatbots can ask users questions, offer suggestions, and guide them through the site, making the experience more engaging and user-friendly.
    - **Efficient Lead Generation**: Chatbots can collect user information through casual

conversation, qualifying leads by asking questions related to user interests or needs. This data can then be sent directly to the sales team for follow-up.

- **Top Chatbot Tools**:
    - **Intercom**: A popular tool for customer support and lead generation, Intercom's AI-powered chatbot offers automated responses, targeted messages, and personalized interactions.
    - **Drift**: Known for its conversational marketing capabilities, Drift uses AI to qualify leads, answer questions, and book meetings with sales representatives, helping streamline the sales funnel.
    - **HubSpot Chatbot**: HubSpot's chatbot builder allows users to create customized chatbots that integrate seamlessly with the HubSpot CRM, making it easy to track interactions and nurture leads.

2. Enhancing Personalization with Virtual Assistants

Virtual assistants offer a more sophisticated level of interaction than standard chatbots, using AI to understand context, track user preferences, and personalize responses. By analyzing past interactions, virtual assistants can recommend products, provide tailored support, and even handle complex tasks like scheduling or account management. This high level of personalization enhances user experience and increases the likelihood of conversions.

- **Top Virtual Assistant Tools**:
    - **IBM Watson Assistant**: Known for its advanced NLP capabilities, Watson Assistant can provide personalized answers, handle complex queries, and integrate with other platforms, such as CRM systems and IoT devices.
    - **Google Dialogflow**: Dialogflow uses Google's machine learning technology to create virtual assistants that understand context, making it ideal for complex, conversation-based interactions. It's widely used for multi-channel support, including websites, apps, and messaging platforms.
    - **Amazon Lex**: Built on the same technology as Alexa, Amazon Lex enables developers to create virtual assistants with voice and text capabilities. It's highly customizable and suitable for managing complex workflows and personalized interactions.

- **Best Practices for Using Virtual Assistants**:
    - **Offer Context-Aware Responses**: Virtual assistants can improve engagement by understanding context. For example, if a returning user asks about a previous order, the assistant can pull up relevant order details and provide

specific updates.
- **Integrate with CRM for Seamless Personalization**: By integrating with your CRM, virtual assistants can personalize interactions based on user data, such as purchase history or browsing behavior. This helps build a seamless, user-centric experience.
- **Encourage Natural Conversation**: Virtual assistants should feel conversational rather than robotic. Use natural language responses and incorporate small talk options to make interactions more enjoyable and relatable.

3. Increasing Engagement and Conversion Through Chatbots and Virtual Assistants

Chatbots and virtual assistants play a crucial role in guiding users along their journey on your site, helping to drive engagement and conversions. By strategically placing these tools on high-traffic pages, you can provide relevant, real-time assistance that keeps users engaged and directs them toward conversion opportunities.

- **Strategies for Driving Engagement and Conversion**:
    - **Guide Users Through the Sales Funnel**: Use chatbots to qualify leads and direct users to appropriate resources, such as product pages, sign-up forms, or

demo requests. This proactive approach helps convert casual visitors into engaged prospects.
- **Provide Assistance on Key Pages**: Place chatbots on landing pages, pricing pages, and checkout pages to answer questions that may prevent users from converting. By addressing potential obstacles, chatbots can reduce abandonment rates and improve conversions.
- **Encourage Return Visits**: Use virtual assistants to personalize messages and recommendations based on previous interactions, encouraging users to return for repeat visits. For example, send follow-up messages or reminders about items left in a shopping cart.

4. Tracking and Optimizing Chatbot and Virtual Assistant Performance

To maximize the effectiveness of chatbots and virtual assistants, it's essential to monitor their performance and make improvements based on user feedback and engagement metrics. Tracking data such as interaction rates, response satisfaction, and conversion impact can provide valuable insights for optimizing user experience.

- **Metrics to Track**:
    - **Engagement Rate**: Measure how often users interact with the chatbot or virtual assistant. High engagement indicates that users find the tool helpful and accessible.
    - **Response Satisfaction**: Use user feedback or post-interaction surveys to gauge satisfaction with the responses provided by the chatbot or virtual assistant.
    - **Conversion Impact**: Analyze the impact of chat interactions on conversions, such as the number of leads generated or the percentage of users who completed a purchase after engaging with the bot.

- **Optimizing Based on Insights**:
    - **Refine Conversational Flow**: Use data from user interactions to refine the bot's conversational flow, ensuring that it aligns with common user needs and queries.
    - **Update Responses Regularly**: Keep chatbot and assistant responses up-to-date with relevant information, especially for time-sensitive queries like promotions, product availability, and policy changes.
    - **Use A/B Testing**: Test different response styles, call-to-action messages, and placement strategies to identify which configurations yield the best results.

Bringing It All Together: Boosting Engagement with AI-Driven Chatbots and Virtual Assistants

AI-powered chatbots and virtual assistants are valuable tools for enhancing user engagement and providing personalized support on your website. By implementing chatbots to handle common inquiries and virtual assistants for more complex, personalized interactions, businesses can create a seamless user experience that keeps visitors engaged, encourages conversions, and builds loyalty. These tools not only improve efficiency but also create meaningful connections with users, making them essential components of a modern, AI-enhanced digital strategy.

Chapter 14. Measuring Success

As artificial intelligence reshapes search engine algorithms and user behavior, measuring SEO success requires a more dynamic, data-driven approach. Traditional metrics like rankings and traffic are still valuable, but understanding success demands a deeper focus on user experience, engagement, and content relevance. AI-driven tools now enable more sophisticated tracking of performance metrics, providing insights into how users interact with content, where conversions happen, and what elements enhance visibility and engagement.

A. Defining New Metrics for AI SEO

Traditional SEO metrics alone no longer provide a complete picture of success. New metrics have emerged to address the unique ways in which AI-driven algorithms assess and rank content. These include AI visibility scores, which gauge a website's relevance and reach in AI-powered search results, and voice search rankings, which measure a site's performance in voice-activated searches. By understanding and tracking these metrics, businesses can adapt to the latest shifts in search behavior and optimize for AI-driven search engines, ensuring that their content remains competitive. Here's an overview of these new metrics and how to integrate them into your SEO strategy.

1. AI Visibility Scores: Measuring Relevance in AI-Powered Results

An AI visibility score provides insight into how effectively your content is reaching users across AI-driven search results, including Google's featured snippets, knowledge panels, and People Also Ask (PAA) sections. AI visibility scores are often calculated by analyzing a site's appearance in rich results, featured content areas, and other enhanced SERP elements that AI-driven algorithms favor.

- **How AI Visibility Scores Work**:
    - **Assess Presence in AI-Enhanced SERPs**: AI visibility scores consider your content's presence in AI-driven SERP features, such as featured snippets, answer boxes, knowledge graphs, and PAA. A higher score indicates a strong presence in these enhanced search elements.
    - **Evaluate Content Relevance and Engagement**: AI visibility scores also account for user engagement metrics like dwell time, click-through rate, and scroll depth, as AI algorithms prioritize content that resonates with users.

- **Top Tools for Tracking AI Visibility Scores**:
    - **SEMrush and Ahrefs**: Both platforms offer tools for tracking visibility in SERP features like featured snippets and PAA boxes, contributing to an overall visibility score.
    - **BrightEdge**: BrightEdge provides an AI-powered content optimization platform that tracks presence in rich snippets and calculates visibility based on reach across different AI-influenced SERP elements.

- **Best Practices for Improving AI Visibility Scores**:
    - **Optimize for Featured Snippets and Rich Results**: Structure content with clear headers, bullet points, and lists to increase chances of appearing in featured snippets and answer boxes.

- **Enhance User Engagement Metrics**: Focus on creating engaging content that keeps users on the page longer, improves readability, and encourages interaction to boost your score in AI-driven search.

2. Voice Search Rankings: Tracking Performance in Voice-Activated Searches

With the growing popularity of voice search, ranking in voice-activated results has become an essential SEO metric. Voice search rankings measure a website's visibility in voice search responses, particularly in devices like Google Assistant, Amazon Alexa, and Apple's Siri, which typically provide only one or two results per query. Optimizing for voice search can improve visibility among users who rely on voice assistants, helping capture a rapidly expanding market.

- **How Voice Search Rankings Work**:
    - **Focus on Conversational, Question-Based Queries**: Voice search rankings are heavily influenced by natural language queries and often prioritize content that answers specific questions succinctly. Ranking in voice search depends on optimizing for common question phrases like "How do I…" or "What is the best…?"
    - **Prioritize Page Speed and Mobile Optimization**: Voice searches are predominantly conducted on mobile devices, making mobile optimization and fast page load times critical for ranking well in voice search results.

- **Top Tools for Tracking Voice Search Rankings**:
    - **Moz and SEMrush**: Both platforms now

include features for tracking keyword rankings specifically for voice search queries, offering insights into how content performs across voice-activated devices.
    - **Answer The Public and Frase**: These tools help identify question-based keywords commonly used in voice search, allowing marketers to optimize for these queries and monitor performance.

- **Best Practices for Improving Voice Search Rankings**:
    - **Use Speakable Schema Markup**: Implement *Speakable* schema on important passages, such as FAQs and summaries, to improve your chances of being selected for voice responses.
    - **Answer Questions Directly and Concisely**: Provide clear, straightforward answers to common questions. Voice assistants favor concise responses that address user queries quickly and accurately.
    - **Focus on Local SEO for "Near Me" Searches**: Many voice searches are location-based, so ensure your content is optimized for local SEO and location-specific queries.

Bringing It All Together: Adapting SEO to AI Metrics

Incorporating AI visibility scores and voice search rankings into your SEO strategy allows you to adapt to the latest shifts in AI-driven search. These metrics provide insights into how effectively your content reaches and engages users across new search environments, helping you stay competitive. By tracking and optimizing for these metrics, you can improve your relevance, expand your reach, and enhance user engagement in both traditional and AI-enhanced search results.

B. Integrating Traditional and AI Metrics

Success depends on a balanced approach that combines traditional SEO metrics with newer AI-influenced measurements. Traditional metrics like organic traffic, keyword rankings, and backlinks remain essential for evaluating the foundational aspects of SEO. However, AI metrics—such as AI visibility scores, voice search rankings, and user engagement indicators—provide insights into how well your content aligns with AI-driven search features and user behavior. A holistic performance measurement strategy integrates these metrics, allowing businesses to adapt to evolving search trends and ensure comprehensive SEO success. Here's how to combine traditional and AI metrics into a unified approach that supports long-term growth and engagement.

1. Combining Traditional SEO Metrics with AI Visibility Metrics

Traditional SEO metrics, such as organic traffic, keyword rankings, and backlink profiles, provide a reliable foundation for understanding search visibility and site authority. When combined with AI visibility scores and engagement metrics, they offer a more comprehensive view of how content performs across both conventional and AI-enhanced search environments.

- **Key Traditional Metrics to Track**:
    - **Organic Traffic**: Organic traffic from search engines reflects the overall visibility and appeal of your content, showing how well it attracts clicks from SERPs.
    - **Keyword Rankings**: Monitoring keyword rankings for core terms allows you to see where your site stands against competitors and which

keywords drive the most traffic.
- **Backlinks and Domain Authority**: A strong backlink profile and domain authority signal credibility to search engines, impacting overall rankings and visibility.

- **Combining with AI Metrics**:
    - **AI Visibility Scores**: Track your presence in AI-driven SERP features like featured snippets, PAA boxes, and knowledge panels, as these features often bring more visibility and traffic.
    - **Engagement Metrics**: Incorporate AI-focused engagement metrics, such as dwell time and click-through rates, which AI algorithms consider when evaluating content relevance and quality.

- **Best Practices for Integration**:
    - **Balance Quantity and Quality**: While traditional metrics often focus on quantity (e.g., traffic, links), AI metrics emphasize quality (e.g., engagement and relevance). Focus on a blend of high-traffic keywords and engaging content that holds user attention.
    - **Track Consistently Across Platforms**: Use comprehensive tools like Google Analytics, SEMrush, and Ahrefs to track both traditional and AI metrics, ensuring all insights are accessible in one place for easier analysis.

2. Integrating User Engagement and Experience Metrics

User engagement and experience are at the forefront of AI-influenced SEO. Metrics such as dwell time, click-through rate (CTR), bounce rate, and scroll depth provide insights into how effectively your content engages and retains users. Integrating these AI-driven metrics with traditional performance indicators enhances your understanding of content quality and user satisfaction.

- **Key Engagement Metrics to Include**:
    - **Dwell Time and Bounce Rate**: Dwell time (how long a user spends on a page before returning to the search results) and bounce rate (percentage of users who leave after viewing one page) indicate how well your content meets user expectations.
    - **Click-Through Rate (CTR)**: CTR measures the percentage of users who click your link on the SERP, reflecting the relevance and appeal of your meta titles and descriptions.
    - **Scroll Depth and Interaction Rate**: Monitoring how far users scroll on a page or engage with elements (e.g., clicking links, watching videos) helps you assess content structure and interactivity.

- **Combining with Traditional User Metrics**:
    - **Page Views and Session Duration**: Page views and session duration provide a baseline for user interest, while engagement metrics give a more nuanced view of content effectiveness.
    - **Conversion Rates and Lead Generation**: Track conversions and leads generated by specific content pieces or pages, combining these with engagement data to see which types of content lead to meaningful user actions.

- **Best Practices for Integration**:
    - **Optimize Content for Engagement**: Focus on creating content that both attracts clicks (CTR) and keeps users engaged (dwell time,

scroll depth). This approach aligns with both traditional and AI metrics, improving rankings and engagement.
    - **Use A/B Testing**: Experiment with variations in meta descriptions, headlines, and CTAs to increase CTR and engagement, using data from both AI and traditional metrics to measure results.

3. Tracking Voice and Mobile-Specific Metrics

Voice and mobile search have become central, where user behavior and preferences are often different than in traditional desktop searches. Voice search rankings and mobile usability metrics are crucial for understanding how your content performs in these formats.

- **Key Metrics for Voice and Mobile Optimization**:
    - **Voice Search Rankings**: Monitor performance for question-based, conversational queries commonly used in voice searches.
    - **Mobile Page Speed and Core Web Vitals**: Google's Core Web Vitals—focused on loading speed, interactivity, and visual stability—are particularly important for mobile search performance.
    - **Mobile Bounce Rate**: Mobile bounce rate reflects how well your content retains users on smartphones, indicating mobile-friendly layout and readability.

- **Combining with Traditional Mobile Metrics**:
    - **Mobile Traffic Share**: Track the proportion of traffic coming from mobile devices to understand user preferences and allocate resources accordingly.
    - **Conversion Rate on Mobile**: Monitor how

well mobile users convert compared to desktop users, as optimizing the mobile experience can improve conversions across mobile devices.

- **Best Practices for Integration**:
    - **Optimize for Conversational Content**: Create content that is conversational and aligns with common voice search queries, improving visibility in both text and voice formats.
    - **Use Structured Data for Enhanced Mobile and Voice Results**: Implement schema markup like FAQ and How-To schema to improve mobile and voice search visibility and help content appear in rich results.

Bringing It All Together: A Unified Approach to SEO Performance

By integrating traditional and AI-driven SEO metrics, you can develop a holistic approach to performance measurement that addresses both foundational SEO principles and the latest trends in AI-driven search. This balanced perspective allows you to track visibility, engagement, and conversions across various search environments, ensuring a well-rounded strategy that adapts to user needs and technological shifts. Combining these metrics enables a more comprehensive and data-informed approach to SEO, equipping you to make strategic adjustments, optimize for AI-driven search features, and maintain a competitive edge.

C. Tools for Monitoring AI SEO Performance

As AI continues to shape SEO, monitoring performance requires tools that can track both traditional metrics and AI-specific indicators, such as visibility in rich snippets, voice search rankings, and user engagement patterns. Specialized software and platforms designed for AI SEO provide insights into how your content performs across AI-enhanced search environments and help you adjust strategies to meet evolving algorithms and user behavior. Here's an overview of essential tools for monitoring AI SEO performance, focusing on software that integrates traditional metrics with AI-specific insights for a comprehensive view.

1. Advanced SEO and Analytics Platforms

These platforms provide robust solutions for tracking traditional and AI-specific SEO metrics, offering a comprehensive view of performance across all search environments. They combine visibility scores, SERP tracking, and engagement analytics, allowing marketers to stay informed on how their content ranks, engages, and converts.

- **SEMrush**:
    - **Overview**: SEMrush is an all-in-one SEO tool that tracks rankings, backlinks, organic traffic, and more. It also includes features for monitoring visibility in rich results, such as featured snippets and PAA boxes, which are prioritized in AI-driven search.
    - **AI-Relevant Features**: The Position Tracking tool monitors keywords in featured snippets, voice search rankings, and local search visibility. SEMrush also offers engagement metrics like click-through rate (CTR) and dwell time, essential for assessing AI SEO performance.
    - **Best Use**: Ideal for tracking a comprehensive set of metrics, SEMrush is valuable for teams seeking insights into traditional SEO metrics

alongside AI visibility.

- **Ahrefs**:
    - **Overview**: Ahrefs is known for its powerful backlink analysis, keyword research, and competitor tracking capabilities. It offers rich insights into keyword rankings and domain authority, along with visibility in various SERP features.
    - **AI-Relevant Features**: Ahrefs tracks featured snippet rankings and monitors keywords that appear in People Also Ask sections, both of which contribute to AI visibility scores. It also provides detailed engagement metrics and competitor comparisons.
    - **Best Use**: Ahrefs is excellent for monitoring visibility in AI-powered SERP features and is particularly useful for backlink analysis and competitor insights.

- **BrightEdge**:
    - **Overview**: BrightEdge is an enterprise-level platform focused on data-driven content and SEO. It provides extensive tracking for keywords, content performance, and user engagement, tailored to large-scale SEO strategies.
    - **AI-Relevant Features**: BrightEdge uses AI to monitor SERP visibility across rich snippets, PAA boxes, and other enhanced features. It also includes advanced analytics for voice search rankings and localized search results.
    - **Best Use**: Suitable for enterprises with complex SEO needs, BrightEdge is best for companies aiming to optimize large volumes of content and track visibility in AI-driven search features.

2. Voice Search Optimization Tools

Voice search optimization tools help track performance in voice-activated searches, monitor how your content ranks in response to voice queries, and identify improvements to better align with spoken search behavior. These tools are particularly useful for businesses optimizing for smart speakers and mobile voice assistants.

- **Answer The Public**:
    - **Overview**: Answer The Public is a keyword research tool that specializes in question-based and conversational keyword data, which aligns with voice search patterns.
    - **AI-Relevant Features**: The tool surfaces common questions and phrases users search for, enabling marketers to target voice-activated queries. It reveals trending questions and "how-to" searches, ideal for voice search optimization.
    - **Best Use**: Useful for content teams seeking to optimize for conversational, question-based queries commonly used in voice search.

- **Moz**:
    - **Overview**: Moz is a well-known SEO tool with strong features for keyword tracking, link building, and local SEO. Recently, Moz has added capabilities for tracking voice search rankings.
    - **AI-Relevant Features**: Moz provides insights into voice-friendly keywords and monitors rankings specifically for voice search queries. It also offers local SEO optimization, which is valuable for "near me" and location-based voice searches.
    - **Best Use**: Best for companies focusing on both voice search and local SEO, especially for capturing mobile and voice-activated search traffic.

- **Frase**:
    - **Overview**: Frase is an AI-driven content optimization tool designed to help marketers create content that answers user questions, particularly in the context of voice search.
    - **AI-Relevant Features**: Frase identifies question-based keywords and provides content recommendations for structuring answers that are optimized for voice search. It also uses AI to analyze competitor content and improve relevance in voice search results.
    - **Best Use**: Ideal for content creators focused on question-based content that aligns with voice search, Frase is well-suited for improving voice search visibility and engagement.

3. User Behavior and Engagement Analytics Tools

User engagement analytics tools provide deeper insights into how users interact with your site, content, and SERP features. Metrics like dwell time, scroll depth, and interaction rate are crucial for assessing how well your content resonates with users, especially as AI algorithms increasingly prioritize engagement.

- **Hotjar**:
    - **Overview**: Hotjar is a behavior analytics tool that visualizes user engagement through heatmaps, session recordings, and user feedback.
    - **AI-Relevant Features**: Hotjar's heatmaps and session recordings reveal how users interact with AI-enhanced content, such as rich snippets and voice-optimized content. It also provides feedback from users, allowing for continuous improvement based on real user experience.

- **Best Use**: Best for teams focused on understanding user engagement and refining content layout based on user interaction patterns.

- **Crazy Egg**:
    - **Overview**: Crazy Egg is another behavior analytics platform with features like heatmaps, A/B testing, and scroll tracking to analyze user interaction.
    - **AI-Relevant Features**: Crazy Egg's scroll tracking and A/B testing are useful for optimizing content structure and engagement. These insights can help refine content for AI-driven engagement metrics like dwell time and scroll depth.
    - **Best Use**: Useful for optimizing user experience and increasing content engagement, Crazy Egg is ideal for testing and refining page layouts to align with AI-driven engagement priorities.

- **Google Analytics 4 (GA4)**:
    - **Overview**: Google Analytics 4 is Google's latest analytics platform, designed to provide insights into both web and app engagement with a focus on predictive metrics.
    - **AI-Relevant Features**: GA4 offers AI-driven insights into predictive user behavior, such as purchase probability and churn likelihood, and integrates engagement metrics like dwell time and scroll depth.
    - **Best Use**: Essential for tracking a wide range of SEO and engagement metrics, GA4 is a core tool for understanding user behavior, tracking conversions, and optimizing for AI-relevant engagement metrics.

Bringing It All Together: Choosing the Right Tools for

AI SEO Monitoring

Integrating specialized AI SEO monitoring tools into your strategy allows you to track performance across traditional and AI-driven metrics effectively. Combining advanced SEO platforms, voice search optimization tools, and behavior analytics tools gives you a well-rounded perspective, helping you understand both the technical and user-driven factors that influence AI SEO success. By monitoring these diverse metrics and using the insights to refine your content, user experience, and engagement strategies, you can stay competitive.

D. Continuous Improvement Strategies

Continuous improvement is essential to maintain competitiveness and adapt to evolving search algorithms. Implementing strategies like Agile SEO, regular audits, and staying updated on the latest trends and algorithm changes can help ensure that your content remains optimized and relevant. These approaches enable SEO teams to respond quickly to new opportunities, address performance issues, and refine strategies based on real-time data. Here's how to leverage Agile SEO, regular audits, and proactive learning for ongoing SEO success.

1. Agile SEO: A Flexible and Iterative Approach

Agile SEO applies the principles of Agile methodology—such as flexibility, iterative improvements, and rapid response to changes—to SEO strategies. By breaking down SEO tasks into smaller, manageable cycles, Agile SEO enables teams to adapt to new insights, respond to algorithm updates, and continually refine content and technical optimization.

- **Core Elements of Agile SEO**:
    - **Short Iterative Cycles**: Divide SEO initiatives into sprints (typically 1–2 weeks) with specific goals, such as optimizing a set of pages or testing a new keyword strategy. This approach allows teams to make small, incremental improvements and measure the impact of each iteration.
    - **Data-Driven Adjustments**: Agile SEO emphasizes regular data analysis and rapid adjustments based on results. For example, if a keyword strategy shows early signs of success, it can be scaled; if it underperforms, adjustments are made before further investments.
    - **Cross-Functional Collaboration**: Agile SEO often involves collaboration between SEO, content, development, and marketing teams, ensuring that all aspects of SEO are aligned and implemented efficiently.

- **Best Practices for Implementing Agile SEO**:
    - **Set Clear Objectives for Each Sprint**: Define measurable goals, such as increasing traffic by a specific percentage or improving rankings for target keywords. This helps keep each iteration focused and results-oriented.
    - **Use A/B Testing to Optimize Quickly**: Agile SEO allows for frequent testing. Use A/B testing for on-page elements like titles, meta descriptions, and CTAs to optimize for better click-through rates (CTR) and engagement.
    - **Evaluate and Refine After Each Sprint**: Review data after each cycle to determine what worked well and what didn't, using these insights to guide future sprints.

2. Regular SEO Audits: Maintaining Technical and

Content Health

Conducting regular SEO audits is essential for identifying areas where your site may need optimization, especially as search engines continually adjust their algorithms. SEO audits evaluate technical performance, content quality, and compliance with current SEO best practices, helping ensure that your site remains in optimal shape for visibility and ranking.

- **Components of an SEO Audit**:
    - **Technical SEO Check**: This includes auditing elements like site speed, mobile usability, indexability, crawlability, and Core Web Vitals. Regular technical checks help maintain a strong foundation for search engines to navigate and rank your site.
    - **Content Quality Review**: Evaluate existing content to ensure it is up-to-date, relevant, and optimized for keywords. Remove or update outdated pages, and ensure content meets E-E-A-T (Experience, Expertise, Authority, Trust) standards.
    - **Backlink Profile Analysis**: Reviewing your backlink profile helps identify both high-quality links and any toxic or low-value backlinks that could harm rankings. Tools like Ahrefs or SEMrush can help with this analysis.

- **Best Practices for Conducting Regular Audits**:
    - **Schedule Quarterly or Biannual Audits**: Regularly auditing your site, whether quarterly or biannually, ensures that any issues are detected early and resolved promptly.
    - **Use Tools to Automate Audits**: Use platforms like Screaming Frog, SEMrush, or Ahrefs to automate parts of the audit process, such as

broken link checks, meta tag analysis, and site speed assessments.
- **Document Findings and Action Items**: Keep a record of each audit's findings and list actionable steps for addressing any issues. This documentation provides a clear roadmap for improvements and accountability within the team.

3. Staying Updated: Proactive Learning and Adaptation

SEO is constantly evolving, with frequent updates to search engine algorithms, new ranking factors, and shifts in user behavior. Staying informed about these changes enables SEO professionals to make proactive adjustments to their strategies and remain competitive. Following SEO news, participating in industry forums, and experimenting with new techniques are essential for continuous improvement.

Ways to Stay Updated:

- **Follow Industry Leaders and Publications**: Regularly read insights from SEO experts and trusted publications, such as Moz, Search Engine Journal, and the Google Search Central Blog. These sources provide timely updates on algorithm changes, ranking trends, and new SEO tools.
- **Participate in Webinars, Conferences, and Courses**: Attending events like MozCon, SMX, and webinars offered by platforms like SEMrush or Ahrefs can provide deeper insights and training in the latest SEO strategies.
- **Join SEO Communities**: Engage in online communities, such as Reddit's SEO subreddit, Slack groups, or LinkedIn groups. These communities offer opportunities to discuss

challenges, share successes, and learn from peers' experiences.

- **Best Practices for Applying New Insights**:
    - **Experiment with New Techniques**: Test new strategies, such as voice search optimization, AI-driven keyword research, or structured data, on a small scale before full implementation. Document results to track what works best for your audience.
    - **Adapt Based on Algorithm Updates**: For example, when Google emphasizes Core Web Vitals, prioritize improving site speed and user experience. Stay flexible and responsive to changes in ranking priorities.
    - **Keep a Log of Changes and Outcomes**: Maintain a record of significant SEO changes, such as new tactics or updates implemented after an algorithm change. Tracking outcomes helps refine strategies and demonstrates SEO progress over time.

Bringing It All Together: Ensuring Continuous Improvement

By adopting Agile SEO, conducting regular audits, and staying updated on industry trends, SEO teams can ensure that their strategies remain effective and aligned with AI-driven algorithm changes. This proactive, iterative approach to SEO supports continuous improvement, enabling businesses to adapt and maintain strong visibility and engagement. Integrating these continuous improvement strategies into your SEO workflow positions your site to succeed in an AI-influenced world, helping you achieve sustainable growth and competitive advantage.

Chapter 15. Future-Proofing Your SEO Strategy

Future-proofing your SEO strategy is essential for long-term success. As search engines increasingly leverage AI to improve user experience and refine algorithms, businesses must be proactive in adapting to new trends, technologies, and user behaviors. Future-proofing means anticipating changes, embracing flexibility, and building a strategy that can withstand shifts in search engine priorities and consumer expectations. In this chapter, we'll explore key practices for staying ahead of the curve, including investing in emerging technologies, focusing on user-centric content, and maintaining a dynamic approach to SEO. By future-proofing your strategy, you can ensure sustainable visibility, engagement, and growth in an AI-driven search ecosystem.

A. Anticipating AI and Search Engine Trends

As AI technology continues to shape search engine algorithms and user experiences, staying ahead of emerging trends is essential for building a resilient SEO strategy. Advances in machine learning are enabling search engines to interpret content, context, and user intent with greater precision, while augmented reality (AR) and virtual reality (VR) are starting to play a role in search results, offering new opportunities for interactive content. By anticipating these developments and integrating them into your SEO strategy, you can better align with search engine priorities and capture emerging markets. Here's a look at how machine learning advancements and AR/VR integration are transforming SEO and how to prepare for these changes.

1. Machine Learning Advancements: Driving Contextual and Intent-Based Search

Machine learning has become a central component of search engines, allowing algorithms to process vast amounts of data and learn from user behavior to deliver increasingly relevant results. Recent developments in machine learning have led to advancements in natural language processing (NLP) and context-based search, enabling search engines to understand search intent more deeply and rank content accordingly.

- **Key Machine Learning Developments in Search**:
    - **Contextual Understanding and BERT**: Google's BERT (Bidirectional Encoder Representations from Transformers) and subsequent models help search engines interpret the context and subtleties of language. These models enable better understanding of user intent, even with complex or conversational queries.
    - **Multitask Unified Model (MUM)**: Google's MUM can understand and process information across languages, text, images, and videos, delivering richer, multimedia-based results. MUM helps search engines answer nuanced questions by gathering information from multiple sources, making it vital to create multimedia content that meets diverse user intents.

- **How to Optimize for Machine Learning Advancements**:
    - **Focus on High-Quality, Intent-Focused Content**: Ensure that each piece of content aligns with a specific search intent (informational, navigational, or transactional)

and provides a comprehensive answer. Use clear, natural language that's easy for both users and machine learning algorithms to understand.
    - **Incorporate Rich Media and Multimedia**: As models like MUM process various content formats, integrating images, videos, and infographics can enhance your site's relevance and boost visibility in multimedia searches.
    - **Leverage Structured Data**: Implement schema markup to help machine learning algorithms understand the context and relationships within your content, enhancing your chances of appearing in rich results and featured snippets.

2. AR/VR Integration: Creating Interactive Search Experiences

As augmented reality and virtual reality gain traction, they are beginning to influence search, especially for industries like e-commerce, real estate, and travel. AR/VR content allows users to interact with products, spaces, or experiences in immersive ways, bringing a new dimension to search results. Search engines are increasingly favoring sites that offer interactive experiences, as they align with users' evolving expectations for engaging content.

- **Examples of AR/VR in Search**:
    - **AR Product Previews**: AR enables users to view 3D models of products in real-world settings, such as trying on virtual clothing or placing furniture in their homes. Google's 3D and AR search features allow users to view certain objects directly in their space through their mobile devices.
    - **Virtual Tours**: VR technology offers users virtual tours of locations, from real estate

listings to vacation destinations. VR content is particularly impactful for industries that benefit from immersive experiences, such as tourism and real estate.

- **How to Optimize for AR/VR Search Integration**:
    - **Create 3D Models for Products**: For e-commerce, consider producing 3D models of popular products to facilitate AR experiences. Tools like Google's ARCore or ARKit can help create models that are compatible with mobile devices, enhancing your visibility in AR search.
    - **Add Virtual Tours to Key Pages**: For industries where physical space matters, such as real estate or hospitality, adding virtual tours can improve user engagement and SEO performance. Platforms like Matterport or YouTube VR enable easy creation and sharing of VR content.
    - **Use Structured Data for AR/VR Content**: To improve visibility, use structured data to help search engines identify and categorize your AR/VR content. Google's "Product" schema, for example, supports AR product experiences, making it easier for search engines to display 3D models in relevant search results.

Bringing It All Together: Preparing for AI and AR/VR Trends

Anticipating machine learning and AR/VR trends helps future-proof your SEO strategy by aligning your content with cutting-edge search technologies. By creating intent-focused, multimedia-rich content and exploring immersive AR/VR options, you position your brand to stay competitive as search engines prioritize engaging, contextually relevant experiences. Staying informed on advancements in machine learning and investing in interactive content can ensure that your site remains adaptable to evolving user expectations and technological shifts in search.

B. Embracing Ethical SEO Practices

Ethical SEO practices are essential not only for compliance but also for building trust with users and search engines alike. As algorithms become more sophisticated and user awareness of data privacy grows, transparency, user privacy, and regulatory compliance are key pillars of sustainable SEO. By adopting ethical practices, businesses can create a positive user experience, align with search engine guidelines, and mitigate risks associated with data misuse or algorithmic penalties. Here's how to embrace transparency, prioritize user privacy, and ensure compliance in your SEO strategy.

1. Transparency: Building Trust Through Honest SEO Practices

Transparency in SEO means clearly representing your brand, intentions, and content to both users and search engines. Misleading tactics, like clickbait, hidden content, or keyword stuffing, may yield short-term gains but can harm trust and damage SEO in the long run. Being upfront and clear in all digital practices not only protects your brand's reputation but also helps build a loyal user base.

- **Key Practices for Transparent SEO**:
    - **Accurate Titles and Meta Descriptions**: Ensure that titles and meta descriptions accurately represent the content on the page. Avoid using clickbait that promises information unrelated to the actual content.

- **User-Friendly URLs**: Use clean, descriptive URLs that reflect the content of each page. This helps users and search engines understand page relevance immediately.
- **Clear Attribution for Sponsored Content**: If your site includes sponsored posts or affiliate links, make it clear to users. Transparency about paid partnerships fosters trust and ensures compliance with search engine guidelines.

- **Best Practices**:
  - **Avoid Manipulative Tactics**: Techniques like hiding keywords or cloaking (showing different content to search engines and users) can lead to penalties. Stick to straightforward, honest SEO practices that align with search engine policies.
  - **Be Consistent with Branding**: Use consistent messaging across meta descriptions, headlines, and content to reinforce transparency and authenticity.

2. User Privacy: Protecting Data and Enhancing User Trust

As privacy regulations evolve and users become more cautious about sharing their personal information, prioritizing user privacy is critical to ethical SEO. Respecting privacy through transparent data collection and usage practices not only keeps you compliant but also improves user trust and engagement.

- **Key Elements of User Privacy in SEO**:
  - **GDPR and CCPA Compliance**: Adhere to privacy regulations like the General Data Protection Regulation (GDPR) in Europe and

the California Consumer Privacy Act (CCPA) in the U.S. These regulations require user consent for data collection and the right to access, delete, or control personal information.
- **Clear Privacy Policies**: Publish a detailed privacy policy that explains what data is collected, how it's used, and the user's rights. This policy should be easily accessible from all pages, ideally linked in the footer.
- **Cookie Consent Banners**: Display a clear consent banner informing users of cookie usage and data tracking. Allow users to opt in or out of non-essential cookies, aligning with privacy regulations.

- **Best Practices**:
  - **Minimize Data Collection**: Collect only the data you truly need, and avoid excessive or intrusive tracking that may compromise user trust.
  - **Encrypt User Data**: Protect sensitive information with HTTPS encryption and data encryption measures. A secure site not only protects users but is also a ranking factor in search engines.

3. Compliance: Adhering to Search Engine and Legal Guidelines

Compliance is fundamental to ethical SEO, encompassing both adherence to search engine guidelines and legal standards. By following these guidelines, businesses protect themselves from penalties, legal actions, and damage to their online reputation. Compliance ensures that your site remains accessible, discoverable, and aligned with evolving standards in SEO and digital marketing.

- **Key Areas of Compliance in SEO**:
    - **Search Engine Guidelines**: Google and other search engines publish SEO guidelines that discourage manipulative practices like link schemes, hidden content, and excessive keyword stuffing. Following these rules keeps your site in good standing and reduces the risk of penalties.
    - **Accessibility Standards (ADA Compliance)**: Ensure your website is accessible to users with disabilities by adhering to Web Content Accessibility Guidelines (WCAG). Use alt tags for images, clear navigation, and screen reader compatibility to make your site accessible to all users.
    - **Data Retention and Management**: Compliance with data retention policies means storing personal data securely and for only as long as necessary. Review and delete unnecessary or outdated data to comply with privacy laws and improve data security.
- **Best Practices**:
    - **Conduct Regular Compliance Audits**: Periodically audit your SEO practices and site content to ensure ongoing compliance with the latest search engine guidelines and legal requirements.
    - **Stay Informed on Regulation Changes**: Privacy and accessibility standards evolve frequently. Stay updated on any changes in privacy laws or SEO guidelines to keep your practices compliant and protect your site from penalties.

Bringing It All Together: Ethical SEO for Long-Term Success

Embracing ethical SEO practices through transparency, user privacy, and compliance is key to creating a sustainable and trustworthy digital presence. By following these principles, you build a foundation of trust with users and search engines, positioning your brand as reputable, reliable, and user-focused. Ethical SEO is not only a way to avoid penalties but also an opportunity to strengthen brand reputation, improve user satisfaction, and ensure long-term success.

C. Building a Culture of Adaptation

Fostering a culture of adaptation within your team is essential for staying competitive. Embracing continuous learning, knowledge sharing, and experimentation allows teams to remain agile, respond to changes quickly, and continuously optimize strategies. Building a culture that prioritizes adaptation equips teams with the tools, mindset, and skills needed to thrive in a dynamic environment. Here's how training, knowledge sharing, and experimentation can help create a culture of adaptation in your SEO strategy.

1. Training: Keeping Skills Current

SEO and digital marketing are fields that require constant learning due to regular updates in search engine algorithms, advancements in AI, and shifts in user behavior. Ongoing training ensures that your team stays up-to-date with the latest techniques, tools, and best practices. By investing in training, you empower your team with the knowledge needed to adapt and innovate.

- **Approaches to Effective Training**:
  - **Regular Workshops and Courses**: Schedule regular workshops, webinars, or courses on relevant topics such as AI in SEO, new tools, and emerging trends. Platforms like Moz Academy, SEMrush Academy, and LinkedIn Learning offer specialized SEO training modules.
  - **Certifications and Industry Conferences**: Encourage team members to earn certifications (e.g., Google Analytics, SEO certifications) and attend industry conferences such as MozCon, SMX, and BrightonSEO, where they can learn from experts and gain insights on the latest strategies.
  - **Cross-Training Within Departments**: Cross-train team members across different functions (e.g., SEO, content, and analytics) to create a well-rounded understanding of how each area impacts SEO. This approach promotes collaboration and enables team members to take on versatile roles when needed.
- **Best Practices for Fostering a Learning Environment**:
  - **Set Training Goals**: Establish clear learning objectives for each team member, focusing on skills that align with the team's goals and address evolving SEO needs.
  - **Encourage Continuous Improvement**: Create an environment where employees are encouraged to actively seek learning opportunities and stay informed about SEO advancements.

2. Knowledge Sharing: Creating a Collaborative and Informed Team

Knowledge sharing is crucial for building a team that learns and grows together. By openly sharing insights, results, and learnings from past projects or experiments, team members can build on each other's successes and avoid repeating mistakes. Knowledge sharing also fosters a collaborative culture where everyone is aligned with the same goals and objectives.

- **Methods for Knowledge Sharing**:
    - **Weekly or Monthly SEO Roundtables**: Host regular meetings where team members share updates, new insights, and recent SEO trends. These sessions can cover topics like algorithm changes, case studies, and successful campaigns, allowing the entire team to learn from recent experiences.
    - **Documenting and Sharing Best Practices**: Create a centralized repository (e.g., a shared document or knowledge base) with detailed SEO best practices, guides, and process documentation. This repository serves as a resource for both new hires and seasoned team members.
    - **Internal Newsletters or Updates**: Develop an internal newsletter to highlight recent SEO insights, tool updates, or significant changes in search engine guidelines. This keeps the team informed and engaged with the latest developments.

- **Best Practices for Fostering Knowledge Sharing**:
    - **Encourage Open Communication**: Create an environment where team members feel comfortable sharing their insights and asking questions. An open communication culture ensures that everyone benefits from individual learnings and insights.
    - **Celebrate Successful Strategies**: Recognize

and share successful SEO projects or strategies with the team to boost morale and reinforce effective practices.

3. Experimentation: Adapting to Change Through Testing and Innovation

Experimentation enables SEO teams to test new ideas, validate strategies, and quickly adapt to changes. By encouraging a data-driven approach to testing and innovation, you create a team that is comfortable exploring new tactics and refining strategies based on real-world results.

- **Types of SEO Experiments**:
    - **A/B Testing on Meta Titles, Descriptions, and CTAs**: Test different versions of meta titles, descriptions, or CTAs to determine which variations drive higher click-through rates and engagement. This allows your team to identify what resonates best with users and adjust accordingly.
    - **Content Structure and Keyword Optimization Tests**: Experiment with different content structures, keyword placements, and heading styles to see how changes affect rankings and user engagement. Testing variations can provide insights into the most effective content optimizations for both users and search engines.
    - **User Experience (UX) Tests for Engagement**: Conduct tests to optimize UX elements, such as navigation, page speed, and mobile responsiveness, and assess their impact on SEO metrics like dwell time and bounce rate. Improving these elements helps create a better user experience, which is increasingly important

in AI-driven SEO.

- **Best Practices for Fostering a Culture of Experimentation:**
    - **Encourage Small-Scale Tests**: Begin with small-scale experiments on a limited set of pages or keywords. This approach allows for quicker results without large-scale risks.
    - **Track and Analyze Results**: Document each experiment's outcomes, capturing key data points and insights. Review results with the team to discuss what worked, what didn't, and how future experiments can be improved.
    - **Foster a Growth Mindset**: Encourage team members to view both successful and unsuccessful experiments as learning opportunities. A growth mindset promotes innovation and continuous improvement, keeping your team adaptable and resilient.

Bringing It All Together: Creating a Dynamic and Adaptable SEO Team

Building a culture of adaptation through training, knowledge sharing, and experimentation empowers SEO teams to stay competitive and agile in a constantly evolving environment. By investing in ongoing education, encouraging collaboration, and embracing a test-and-learn mindset, you equip your team with the tools needed to respond effectively to changes in AI-driven search algorithms and user expectations. Cultivating an adaptive culture enables your SEO strategy to remain resilient, innovative, and prepared for future developments.

D. Collaboration with AI and Tech Partners

As AI and technology become increasingly integral to SEO, collaborating with specialized AI and tech partners can accelerate innovation, enhance capabilities, and ensure that your SEO strategy remains competitive. By leveraging the expertise of AI-driven firms, data analytics specialists, and tech providers, businesses can access cutting-edge tools, insights, and resources that drive more effective SEO outcomes. Forming strategic partnerships and exploring joint ventures with these experts allows companies to tap into advanced technology solutions that might be difficult to develop in-house. Here's how to make the most of collaborations with AI and tech partners, focusing on leveraging expertise and pursuing joint initiatives.

1. Leveraging Expertise: Accessing Specialized Knowledge and Resources

AI and tech partners bring specialized knowledge, tools, and resources that can elevate your SEO strategy. By collaborating with these experts, your team can access insights and capabilities that go beyond traditional SEO, such as predictive analytics, advanced data processing, and natural language processing (NLP). Leveraging this expertise helps you stay ahead of industry trends and implement sophisticated, data-driven SEO tactics.

- **Types of Expertise to Leverage**:
    - **AI and Machine Learning**: Work with AI firms specializing in machine learning to gain insights into user behavior, predict trends, and optimize content for changing search patterns. Machine learning can also assist with tasks like automated keyword analysis, content generation, and predictive analytics.
    - **Natural Language Processing (NLP)**:

Collaborate with NLP experts to optimize for voice search and conversational queries. NLP-focused partners can help fine-tune content for search engines that prioritize understanding context and user intent, such as Google's BERT and MUM algorithms.
- **Data Analytics and Insights**: Data analytics specialists can provide in-depth insights into user behavior, conversion pathways, and engagement metrics, allowing for a data-driven SEO approach. Partnering with analytics firms enables more accurate data interpretation and helps identify areas for improvement.

- **Best Practices for Leveraging Partner Expertise**:
    - **Establish Clear Goals and KPIs**: Set specific objectives for each collaboration, such as improving engagement metrics or increasing rankings for voice searches. Defining KPIs ensures that both parties are aligned and focused on measurable outcomes.
    - **Encourage Knowledge Transfer**: Arrange workshops, training sessions, or collaborative projects where partners can share their expertise with your in-house team. This transfer of knowledge strengthens your team's capabilities and promotes long-term growth.
    - **Integrate Technology with Existing Tools**: Work closely with partners to integrate new AI tools and data sources with your existing tech stack, such as Google Analytics, SEMrush, or Ahrefs, to streamline workflows and improve efficiency.

2. Joint Ventures: Exploring Collaborative Projects for Mutual Benefit

Joint ventures with AI and tech partners allow businesses to undertake ambitious projects that benefit both parties, such as co-developing tools, launching pilot programs, or researching emerging trends. These collaborative efforts can help your business achieve more innovative SEO solutions and give your partners an opportunity to expand their capabilities in real-world applications.

- **Examples of Joint Venture Projects**:
    - **Co-Developing AI-Driven SEO Tools**: Work with a tech partner to create proprietary AI-powered SEO tools tailored to your business needs. For example, a joint venture could develop a predictive analytics tool that provides keyword recommendations based on seasonality, user trends, or other unique factors relevant to your audience.
    - **Testing Emerging Technologies in Real-World Scenarios**: Launch pilot programs with partners to test emerging technologies, such as AI-driven content personalization or augmented reality (AR) for e-commerce SEO. Joint ventures that explore new tech applications offer valuable insights and help position your business as an innovator.
    - **Research and Development in User Behavior Modeling**: Collaborate on R&D projects that study user behavior patterns and how they impact SEO. This could include testing different content formats, voice search optimization, or personalization algorithms, and using the findings to refine both SEO strategy and AI models.

- **Best Practices for Successful Joint Ventures**:
    - **Define Mutual Benefits and Roles**: Establish clear roles, responsibilities, and expected outcomes for both parties. Joint ventures should align with each partner's strengths and interests, ensuring that both benefit from the project.
    - **Develop a Long-Term Vision**: While pilot programs and tests provide short-term insights, consider how joint ventures can evolve over time. For example, a co-developed AI tool could initially serve your business but later be adapted and scaled for broader industry use.
    - **Share Results and Apply Insights**: After each collaborative project, document the outcomes and key learnings. Apply these insights to future SEO strategies, and encourage partners to share feedback that could further enhance your joint initiatives.

3. Integrating AI and Tech Partnerships into SEO Strategy

Working closely with AI and tech partners means that their expertise and tools can become an integral part of your SEO workflow. Integrating these partnerships into your SEO strategy helps ensure that your team can seamlessly leverage new technologies and stay adaptable in the face of rapid industry change.

- **Steps to Integrate Partnerships into SEO Strategy**:
    - **Collaborate on Strategy Development**: Engage partners during SEO strategy planning to identify areas where their tools and insights can have the greatest impact. This integration can inform decisions on content optimization,

technical SEO improvements, or user engagement enhancements.
- **Use Partner Technology in Day-to-Day Operations**: Once tools or techniques have been developed, incorporate them into daily SEO processes. For instance, machine learning tools can automate routine tasks like keyword clustering or data analysis, freeing your team to focus on strategic initiatives.
- **Track and Report Impact**: Measure the results of using partner technology, such as improvements in rankings, traffic, or engagement, and report these metrics back to both internal stakeholders and partners. This helps evaluate the effectiveness of the collaboration and identifies areas for future improvement.

- **Best Practices for Integration**:
  - **Maintain Open Communication**: Establish regular check-ins with partners to discuss progress, challenges, and upcoming goals. Transparent communication ensures that both teams stay aligned and adapt to any changes in priorities.
  - **Encourage In-House Innovation with Partner Support**: Foster a culture of experimentation by using AI and tech partners as support for in-house innovation projects. Encourage team members to explore new SEO tactics and use partner expertise to guide or enhance these efforts.
  - **Evaluate Partnership ROI**: Periodically assess the ROI of each partnership by analyzing improvements in SEO metrics directly attributable to the collaboration. This helps determine the value of the partnership and guides decisions about future investments.

Bringing It All Together: Maximizing the Benefits of AI and Tech Partnerships

Collaboration with AI and tech partners enables businesses to leverage specialized expertise, develop innovative solutions, and stay competitive. By integrating partners into your strategy, pursuing joint ventures, and focusing on knowledge sharing, you can create a powerful, adaptable SEO approach that incorporates the latest advancements in AI and technology.

These partnerships not only enhance your immediate capabilities but also foster a culture of continuous learning and innovation within your organization, ensuring long-term success in an AI-driven digital world.

Chapter 16. Actionable Steps and Implementation Plans

Transforming an SEO strategy requires clear, actionable steps and a well-structured implementation plan. After exploring advanced techniques, ethical practices, adaptive processes, and collaborative partnerships, it's essential to translate these insights into practical initiatives that your team can follow. This chapter provides a roadmap for putting your SEO strategy into action, covering essential steps to guide implementation, ensure accountability, and drive measurable results. By following these structured plans, you can seamlessly integrate new tools, optimize workflows, and achieve sustainable growth in an evolving digital environment.

A. Conducting a Comprehensive SEO Audit

A comprehensive SEO audit is the foundation for any successful SEO strategy, providing insights into your website's strengths, areas for improvement, and optimization opportunities. An audit helps assess technical performance, content quality, user experience, and alignment with AI-driven search priorities. By following a structured checklist and leveraging powerful tools, you can identify issues that may be hindering your site's visibility and engagement and create a clear path forward for improvements. Here's a checklist and recommended tools to guide you through a thorough SEO audit.

1. Technical SEO Audit Checklist

The technical aspects of your site are critical for ensuring that search engines can crawl, index, and display your content effectively. A technical audit reveals issues like slow loading times, crawl errors, and mobile usability challenges that can impact rankings.

- **Checklist for Technical SEO**:
    - **Crawlability**: Check for errors that prevent search engines from crawling and indexing your site. Use tools to identify broken links, orphan pages, and blocked resources.
    - **Page Speed and Core Web Vitals**: Ensure your site meets Google's Core Web Vitals standards, focusing on loading speed, interactivity, and visual stability.
    - **Mobile-Friendliness**: Verify that your site is responsive and optimized for mobile devices, as mobile usability is essential for ranking in mobile-first indexing.
    - **HTTPS and Security**: Confirm that your site uses HTTPS encryption, and check for other security features like safe browsing and data encryption to build trust with users.
    - **Structured Data**: Review your schema markup to ensure that structured data is implemented correctly, improving the likelihood of appearing in rich results.

- **Recommended Tools**:
    - **Google Search Console**: Offers insights into crawl errors, indexing issues, and Core Web Vitals performance.
    - **Screaming Frog SEO Spider**: Crawls your site to identify technical issues such as broken links, duplicate content, and missing metadata.
    - **PageSpeed Insights**: Analyzes page loading speed and Core Web Vitals, providing recommendations for improvement.

2. Content Quality and On-Page SEO Audit Checklist

High-quality, optimized content is essential for ranking well and engaging users. An on-page content audit helps you assess keyword usage, relevance, and user intent alignment, ensuring that your content is up-to-date, valuable, and optimized for AI-driven search engines.

- **Checklist for Content and On-Page SEO**:
    - **Keyword Optimization**: Ensure primary and secondary keywords are incorporated naturally in titles, headings, and throughout the content.
    - **Content Relevance and Value**: Review each page for relevance to user queries, ensuring that content addresses current user needs and includes accurate, useful information.
    - **Internal Linking**: Check that internal links guide users to other valuable resources on your site, improving navigation and spreading link equity.
    - **Meta Tags and Headers**: Review and optimize meta titles, descriptions, and header tags (H1, H2, etc.) for clarity, keyword focus, and clickability.
    - **Image Optimization**: Ensure images have descriptive alt text, appropriate file sizes, and relevant filenames to improve SEO and accessibility.

- **Recommended Tools**:
    - **Ahrefs or SEMrush**: Analyze keyword performance, content relevance, and on-page SEO elements like headings, meta tags, and keyword density.
    - **Grammarly and Hemingway Editor**: Assess readability, grammar, and style to ensure content is clear, concise, and user-friendly.

- **Yoast SEO** (for WordPress): Provides a checklist for optimizing on-page SEO elements and readability.

3. User Experience (UX) and Engagement Audit Checklist

User experience plays an increasingly important role in SEO, with search engines favoring sites that provide a positive, engaging experience. A UX audit helps you optimize navigation, layout, and content structure to improve engagement metrics like dwell time and bounce rate.

- **Checklist for UX and Engagement**:
    - **Site Navigation and Layout**: Evaluate site structure, ensuring users can easily find what they're looking for. Pages should be organized intuitively with clear menus and a logical hierarchy.
    - **Content Readability**: Check that text is easy to read, with sufficient font sizes, spacing, and formatting that encourages users to stay on the page.
    - **Interactive Elements**: Assess interactive elements like forms, calls-to-action (CTAs), and multimedia to ensure they load quickly and function correctly.
    - **Scroll Depth and Engagement Metrics**: Analyze scroll depth, dwell time, and bounce rate to identify content that needs adjustments for improved engagement.
    - **Accessibility**: Ensure compliance with accessibility standards (WCAG) by checking for alt text, keyboard navigation, and screen reader compatibility.

- **Recommended Tools**:
    - **Hotjar or Crazy Egg**: Provides heatmaps and session recordings to visualize user behavior and engagement patterns on your site.
    - **Google Analytics**: Tracks engagement metrics, including bounce rate, average session duration, and pages per session, helping you gauge overall user experience.
    - **Lighthouse**: A Google tool that audits accessibility, performance, and SEO factors to improve user experience and engagement.

4. Off-Page SEO and Backlink Profile Audit Checklist

Off-page SEO factors, including backlinks and brand mentions, play a vital role in building authority and credibility. A backlink audit identifies valuable backlinks, as well as any potentially harmful links that could negatively impact your site's reputation.

- **Checklist for Off-Page SEO**:
    - **Backlink Quality**: Review your backlink profile to ensure links come from reputable, relevant sources that strengthen your site's authority.
    - **Anchor Text Diversity**: Check for a healthy variety of anchor texts to avoid over-optimization, which could appear manipulative to search engines.
    - **Toxic Links**: Identify low-quality or toxic backlinks that could harm your SEO and consider using Google's disavow tool to prevent penalties.
    - **Social Signals and Mentions**: Analyze social media engagement and unlinked brand mentions, as these signals can indicate brand visibility and authority.

- **Recommended Tools**:
    - **Ahrefs or Moz**: Analyze your backlink profile, identify link quality, and track new or lost backlinks.
    - **Google Disavow Tool**: Allows you to remove harmful links from your backlink profile, reducing the risk of penalties.
    - **Brand24 or Mention**: Track brand mentions and social signals, helping you identify potential opportunities for link building and off-page SEO improvement.

Bringing It All Together: Conducting and Acting on an SEO Audit

A comprehensive SEO audit allows you to address technical, content, UX, and off-page factors that affect your site's performance, providing a roadmap for improvements. By following this checklist and leveraging these tools, you can identify gaps, optimize critical areas, and make data-driven decisions to strengthen your SEO strategy. Regular audits—conducted quarterly or biannually—will ensure that your site adapts to changing algorithms, remains technically sound, and continues to deliver valuable, engaging content for users and search engines alike.

B. Prioritizing SEO Efforts

With a multitude of potential SEO initiatives to undertake, prioritizing efforts is essential to make efficient use of time and resources. One effective approach is the *Impact vs. Effort Matrix*, a strategic tool that helps SEO teams assess tasks based on their potential impact on SEO performance and the effort required to implement them. By categorizing tasks into different quadrants, teams can focus first on high-impact, low-effort optimizations while planning for larger projects that deliver significant benefits. Here's how to use the Impact vs. Effort Matrix to prioritize SEO efforts effectively.

1. Understanding the Impact vs. Effort Matrix

The Impact vs. Effort Matrix is a simple but powerful grid that divides tasks into four quadrants based on their potential impact on SEO and the effort (time, resources, complexity) needed to implement them. The quadrants are:

- **Quick Wins (High Impact, Low Effort)**: Tasks that deliver a high return with minimal effort, often considered the best starting point. These tasks are efficient to complete and bring immediate SEO benefits.

- **Major Projects (High Impact, High Effort)**: These are substantial undertakings that, while resource-intensive, offer significant long-term gains. Major projects should be planned and executed strategically to maximize their effectiveness.

- **Low-Hanging Fruit (Low Impact, Low Effort)**: Simple tasks with lower impact, which can be completed quickly but may only offer minor SEO improvements. These tasks are useful for keeping momentum but should not take precedence over more impactful optimizations.

- **Time-Intensive Investments (Low Impact, High Effort)**: Tasks that require a lot of effort but offer minimal benefit to SEO. These are often low-priority and may be postponed or avoided if resources are limited.

2. Applying the Matrix to Common SEO Tasks

Here's how different SEO tasks might fit into each quadrant

of the Impact vs. Effort Matrix:

- **Quick Wins**:
    - **Optimizing Meta Tags and Descriptions**: Updating meta titles and descriptions for clarity and keyword relevance can increase click-through rates with minimal effort.
    - **Fixing Broken Links**: Identifying and fixing broken internal and external links improves user experience and crawlability with minimal time investment.
    - **Updating Outdated Content**: Refreshing older content with new data or insights can help regain rankings and maintain relevance with minimal effort.

- **Major Projects**:
    - **Site Structure Overhaul**: Restructuring the site for better navigation and hierarchy is resource-intensive but enhances both SEO and user experience.
    - **Creating Comprehensive Content Hubs**: Developing in-depth content clusters for targeted topics improves relevance and authority but requires substantial planning and content creation.
    - **Implementing Advanced Schema Markup**: Adding structured data across the site improves visibility in rich snippets but may require collaboration between content, SEO, and development teams.

- **Low-Hanging Fruit**:
    - **Compressing and Optimizing Images**: Reducing image sizes can improve page load times, offering minor but quick SEO benefits.

- **Checking for Duplicate Content**: Scanning for duplicate content helps prevent minor SEO issues, though it generally offers limited impact on rankings.
            - **Adjusting Internal Link Anchors**: Updating anchor text for existing internal links to improve keyword relevance is easy to implement but may offer only small gains.

    - **Time-Intensive Investments**:
        - **Targeting Extremely Competitive Keywords**: Attempting to rank for high-competition keywords may require considerable content and link-building efforts with limited short-term gains.
        - **Implementing Custom Design Elements for SEO**: Extensive custom design work may improve UX but might not directly impact SEO rankings.
        - **Overhauling Low-Traffic Pages**: Making major updates to pages with little traffic or SEO value can be resource-intensive with minimal immediate return.

3. Using the Matrix to Prioritize Tasks

Once you've categorized tasks, use the matrix to create an actionable priority list. Start with Quick Wins, followed by Major Projects, while using Low-Hanging Fruit to maintain ongoing improvements. Avoid or postpone Time-Intensive Investments unless resources allow or specific goals justify them.

- **Step-by-Step Prioritization**:
    - **Identify Quick Wins**: Begin by addressing high-impact, low-effort tasks to see immediate SEO benefits. These optimizations can boost

site performance quickly with minimal resource allocation.
- **Plan Major Projects**: Schedule high-impact, high-effort projects as strategic initiatives. Break down these projects into smaller phases to manage resources effectively and track progress over time.
- **Address Low-Hanging Fruit as Needed**: These tasks can be tackled in between major initiatives to keep up with minor improvements. While they may not bring significant gains, they contribute to overall site health.
- **Limit Time-Intensive Investments**: Only pursue low-impact, high-effort tasks when they align with specific long-term goals or when resources are available. These tasks should be deprioritized to focus on efforts with higher returns.

4. Tools to Support Prioritization and Task Management

Several tools can support the implementation of the Impact vs. Effort Matrix and help you keep track of SEO priorities effectively.

- **Trello or Asana**: Use these project management tools to organize tasks based on the matrix, assign responsibilities, and set deadlines. You can create lists for each quadrant and move tasks as they progress.
- **Google Analytics and Search Console**: Analyze data to determine which tasks have the potential to drive high impact based on performance metrics like traffic, conversions, and engagement.
- **SEMrush or Ahrefs**: Use these tools to identify SEO issues and measure the potential impact of tasks like keyword optimization, link building, and content

updates.

Bringing It All Together: Implementing the Impact vs. Effort Matrix

The Impact vs. Effort Matrix provides a structured way to prioritize SEO tasks and ensure that your team's resources are spent on initiatives that bring measurable results. By focusing first on Quick Wins, strategically planning Major Projects, and keeping Low-Hanging Fruit in rotation, you can maximize your SEO impact efficiently. Regularly revisiting the matrix allows your team to adjust priorities based on changing goals and search engine updates, keeping your SEO efforts aligned with high-impact outcomes.

C. Creating a Roadmap for AI Integration

Integrating AI into your SEO strategy can significantly enhance your site's performance, drive personalization, and improve efficiency. However, adopting AI is most effective when planned with clear short-term wins and long-term goals in mind. A well-structured roadmap helps prioritize AI initiatives, ensuring you leverage quick, impactful improvements while setting the stage for transformative, future-focused applications. Here's how to build a roadmap for integrating AI into your SEO strategy, balancing immediate gains with strategic long-term investments.

1. Identifying Short-Term Wins for Immediate Impact

Short-term wins are AI applications that are relatively quick to implement and deliver measurable benefits with minimal disruption. These quick gains allow your team to see immediate improvements in SEO performance and build confidence in AI as a valuable tool.

- **Key Short-Term Wins**:
    - **Automated Keyword Research**: Use AI-powered tools to streamline keyword discovery and clustering, enabling quicker content optimization. AI-driven platforms like Ahrefs and SEMrush can automate keyword analysis, identifying high-value terms and intent-based clusters that align with user behavior.
    - **Content Optimization and Recommendations**: Implement AI tools like Clearscope or Surfer SEO to enhance content relevance and structure. These tools use NLP to analyze top-ranking content, providing insights on keyword density, content length, and related topics to boost rankings.
    - **Voice Search Optimization**: Optimize for voice search by identifying conversational keywords and common question phrases. Tools like Answer The Public help identify voice-friendly terms that align with user intent, improving your site's chances of ranking for voice-activated searches.
    - **Automated Reporting and Insights**: AI-driven analytics tools like Google Analytics 4 or custom dashboards can automate regular reporting, summarizing key metrics and identifying performance trends. This saves time and provides actionable insights into SEO results.
- **Steps for Implementing Short-Term Wins**:
    - **Prioritize Low-Effort, High-Impact Tools**: Focus on tools that integrate seamlessly with

your existing workflow and require minimal setup. Identify areas where automation can free up team time, like keyword research or reporting.
- **Test AI Tools on Targeted Campaigns**: Start by applying AI tools to specific SEO campaigns or pages. This approach enables you to evaluate tool effectiveness and measure performance improvements without a full-scale rollout.
- **Set Benchmarks and Track Results**: Define baseline metrics, such as keyword rankings or traffic volume, before implementing each tool. Measure short-term improvements to ensure each tool is delivering its intended impact.

2. Setting Long-Term Goals for Strategic AI Integration

Long-term AI goals focus on building a robust, scalable SEO strategy that leverages advanced AI applications to drive sustained performance and competitiveness. These goals may require more time, resources, or expertise, but their payoff is transformative, positioning your site for ongoing growth.

- **Key Long-Term AI Goals**:
    - **Personalized User Experiences**: Use machine learning to deliver personalized content recommendations based on user behavior and preferences. AI-powered tools like Optimizely or Dynamic Yield analyze user data to suggest relevant content, boosting engagement and retention.
    - **Predictive Analytics for SEO Strategy**: Implement AI-driven predictive analytics to forecast trends, user behavior, and keyword performance. Predictive models can help

your team make data-informed decisions and proactively address content or technical needs based on projected shifts.
    - **AI-Powered Content Creation and Scaling**: Leverage AI for content creation at scale, such as generating product descriptions, FAQs, or metadata. Tools like Jasper and Copy.ai can assist with content creation, maintaining quality while freeing up time for higher-level strategy.
    - **Voice and Visual Search Optimization**: Invest in AI tools for optimizing both voice and visual search capabilities, enabling your site to capture a larger share of emerging search formats. Visual recognition tools like Google Lens can help optimize images, and structured data can improve visibility in voice search results.

- **Steps for Implementing Long-Term Goals**:
    - **Develop a Detailed Implementation Plan**: Outline steps for each long-term initiative, including resource needs, technology requirements, and timelines. Assign team members to specific roles and set clear milestones for achieving each goal.
    - **Invest in Advanced AI Partnerships**: Consider partnering with AI and tech firms to co-develop advanced solutions tailored to your business needs. These partnerships can provide access to cutting-edge technology and expertise in machine learning or predictive analytics.
    - **Monitor and Adjust Based on Data**: Continuously track KPIs for each initiative, adjusting tactics based on performance data and industry trends. An adaptable approach ensures long-term goals remain aligned with evolving SEO priorities and user needs.

3. Building a Timeline for Balanced AI Integration

Creating a balanced timeline helps you achieve a smooth integration, balancing quick gains with ongoing projects that drive significant long-term benefits. A clear timeline also ensures that AI initiatives are rolled out systematically, allowing your team to measure results and refine strategies without overwhelming resources.

- **Phased Timeline for AI Integration**:
    - **Phase 1: Initial Setup and Quick Wins (Months 1-3)**
        - Implement AI-powered keyword research, content optimization, and reporting tools.
        - Track the immediate impact on key metrics, such as rankings, click-through rates, and engagement.
        - Gather feedback from team members to refine tool usage and adjust processes as needed.
    - **Phase 2: Intermediate Goals and Testing (Months 4-6)**
        - Begin testing personalized content recommendations and predictive analytics tools on selected pages.
        - Optimize select pages for voice and visual search, monitoring performance in these areas.
        - Assess tool effectiveness and gather data to inform adjustments or refinements.
    - **Phase 3: Full-Scale Implementation of Long-Term Goals (Months 7-12)**
        - Expand personalized content recommendations and predictive analytics across the entire site.
        - Use AI to scale content creation across multiple content types, such as blog

- posts, product descriptions, and FAQ sections.
- Continue monitoring, optimizing, and adjusting tactics based on performance data and industry changes.

4. Tools and Resources for AI Integration

Several AI-powered tools support both short-term and long-term SEO objectives, making it easier to achieve the immediate wins and sustained growth outlined in your roadmap.

- **Short-Term Tools**:
    - **SEMrush and Ahrefs**: For automated keyword research and SERP analysis.
    - **Surfer SEO and Clearscope**: For content optimization based on top-ranking competitor analysis.
    - **Answer The Public**: For identifying conversational queries that support voice search optimization.

- **Long-Term Tools**:
    - **Optimizely and Dynamic Yield**: For AI-driven personalization and user experience improvements.
    - **Google Cloud AI and IBM Watson**: For predictive analytics and advanced machine learning capabilities.
    - **Jasper and Copy.ai**: For AI-assisted content creation, particularly useful for scaling content production.

Bringing It All Together: Implementing the AI Integration Roadmap

A clear roadmap for AI integration, with distinct short-term wins and long-term goals, enables your SEO strategy to evolve efficiently and effectively. By prioritizing immediate AI applications, you can enhance performance with quick, impactful changes, while investing in advanced AI projects that support sustainable growth and competitiveness. Monitoring results, refining tactics, and remaining adaptable ensures that AI continues to deliver value and keeps your SEO strategy ahead of evolving industry trends.

D. Allocating Resources Effectively

Efficiently allocating resources is essential for successfully integrating AI into your SEO strategy. Budgeting, defining team roles, and considering outsourcing options ensure that projects are executed smoothly and that your team is equipped to maximize the impact of AI-driven initiatives. With careful planning, you can manage costs, leverage team strengths, and strategically involve external experts where needed. Here's a guide on how to allocate resources effectively for AI-powered SEO efforts, focusing on budgeting, team roles, and outsourcing options.

1. Budgeting for AI-Driven SEO Initiatives

Budgeting is the foundation of resource allocation, helping you prioritize spending and ensure that funds are distributed to high-impact projects. AI-powered SEO can involve various costs, including software subscriptions, training, and potential consulting fees. Establishing a clear budget ensures that resources are directed toward initiatives that deliver measurable returns.

- **Budgeting Considerations**:
    - **Tool and Software Subscriptions**: AI-powered tools, such as SEMrush, Ahrefs, and

Clearscope, often come with monthly or annual subscription fees. Budget for essential tools first, and add advanced tools as needed based on the scope of your AI integration.
- **Training and Skill Development**: Invest in training to ensure your team can effectively use AI tools and understand their impact on SEO. Budget for online courses, workshops, and certifications, which can be particularly valuable if your team is new to AI-driven SEO.
- **Consulting and Partnership Fees**: If collaborating with AI specialists or tech firms, allocate funds for consulting or partnership fees. These collaborations can be critical for complex projects like predictive analytics or machine learning applications.
- **Content and Production Costs**: Budget for content creation, especially if using AI to scale production. Include costs for AI-assisted writing tools and human editors to maintain quality across generated content.

- **Best Practices for Budgeting**:
  - **Prioritize High-Impact Tools and Initiatives**: Begin by allocating budget to the most impactful tools and projects, focusing on those that deliver high ROI. For example, content optimization tools and predictive analytics typically yield immediate benefits.
  - **Set a Contingency Fund**: Include a small contingency in your budget for unexpected costs, such as additional training needs, tool upgrades, or consulting fees, to allow for flexibility.
  - **Review Budget Periodically**: Regularly assess budget allocation based on performance metrics to ensure resources are being used effectively and adjust as necessary.

2. Defining Team Roles for AI-Driven SEO

Clearly defining team roles ensures that each aspect of your AI-driven SEO strategy has dedicated focus and expertise. By assigning specific responsibilities to team members, you create a structured workflow that enhances accountability and efficiency. Roles may include SEO strategists, content creators, data analysts, and technology specialists, each contributing unique skills to AI integration.

- **Key Roles and Responsibilities**:
    - **SEO Strategist**: The strategist oversees the overall SEO plan, including AI initiatives. This role involves setting objectives, tracking progress, and ensuring that AI tools align with broader SEO goals.
    - **Content Creator**: Content creators and editors produce, optimize, and manage content. They work closely with AI content tools, ensuring that generated content meets quality standards and aligns with SEO goals.
    - **Data Analyst**: Analysts interpret data from AI tools, providing insights into performance metrics, trends, and user behavior. This role is essential for understanding the impact of predictive analytics and user behavior modeling.
    - **Technical SEO Specialist**: The technical SEO specialist ensures that AI integrations are compatible with the site's structure and technical requirements. This role involves implementing structured data, managing site speed, and optimizing for voice and visual search.
    - **AI and Automation Specialist**: For advanced projects, an AI specialist manages machine learning applications and complex integrations.

This role may be outsourced or collaborative with an AI consulting firm, depending on project scope.

- **Best Practices for Role Allocation**:
  - **Define Responsibilities Based on Skillsets**: Assign roles based on each team member's expertise, ensuring that everyone works on tasks suited to their strengths. For instance, content creators should handle AI content tools, while technical SEO specialists focus on backend optimizations.
  - **Encourage Collaboration Between Roles**: Create cross-functional workflows where strategists, analysts, and content creators can collaborate. For example, the SEO strategist and data analyst might work together to prioritize content topics based on predictive analytics.
  - **Provide Training to Enhance AI Proficiency**: Offer specialized training for team members, especially those working directly with AI tools, to ensure they're well-versed in using AI effectively for SEO purposes.

3. Exploring Outsourcing Options for Specialized Needs

Outsourcing certain tasks can be a cost-effective solution, especially for projects that require specialized skills or advanced AI expertise. By outsourcing complex AI applications or niche SEO tasks, you can access expertise without the long-term commitment of additional hires, allowing your core team to focus on strategic and operational goals.

- **Commonly Outsourced SEO Tasks**:

- **AI and Machine Learning Consulting**: For advanced AI applications like predictive analytics, partnering with an AI consultant or data science firm can help manage complex integrations and ensure data accuracy.
- **Content Creation and Optimization**: Outsource specific content projects, especially when scaling up production, to agencies or freelancers experienced with AI-driven content tools. This helps maintain content flow without overwhelming your internal team.
- **Technical SEO Audits and Implementations**: Technical SEO agencies can assist with advanced tasks like site architecture optimization, structured data implementation, or Core Web Vitals improvements, ensuring your site meets SEO requirements.
- **Data Analysis and Predictive Modeling**: Partner with analytics experts to interpret AI-generated insights, model user behavior, and provide data-driven recommendations. This is particularly useful for businesses without in-house data analysts.

- **Best Practices for Outsourcing**:
  - **Vet Vendors Carefully**: Choose vendors with experience in AI and SEO, ideally with case studies or references that demonstrate their expertise. Prioritize those with industry-relevant experience to ensure a smooth collaboration.
  - **Set Clear Expectations and KPIs**: Clearly define project goals, timelines, and key performance indicators (KPIs) to ensure vendors understand your objectives and deliver results that meet your expectations.
  - **Maintain Communication**: Schedule periodic check-ins to discuss progress, provide feedback, and make adjustments as needed.

Open communication helps vendors stay aligned with your goals.

4. Balancing In-House and Outsourced Resources

Finding the right balance between in-house and outsourced resources is essential to maximize productivity and keep costs manageable. By handling core SEO functions internally and outsourcing specialized tasks, you can leverage the strengths of both approaches.

- **Steps to Balance Resources**:
    - **Start with In-House Capabilities**: Begin by identifying tasks your team can handle internally, such as content creation, keyword research, and reporting. This allows your team to retain control over core SEO elements.
    - **Outsource High-Skill, Low-Frequency Tasks**: For tasks that require specialized skills but are not frequently needed, like technical audits or machine learning applications, consider outsourcing. This allows you to access expertise without a permanent commitment.
    - **Allocate Budget According to Priorities**: Direct more budget to core tasks that are handled internally, while setting aside funds for outsourcing specific, high-impact projects. This approach ensures that in-house efforts are well-supported while outsourcing remains cost-effective.

Bringing It All Together: Optimizing Resource Allocation for AI-Driven SEO

Effective resource allocation in AI-driven SEO involves a balanced approach to budgeting, team roles, and outsourcing. By carefully budgeting for essential tools, defining clear roles, and strategically outsourcing specialized tasks, you can maximize your team's efficiency and the impact of your AI initiatives. This structured approach allows you to pursue high-priority projects confidently, integrating AI into your SEO strategy without overwhelming internal resources.

Chapter 17. Case Studies and Real-World Applications

Reviewing case studies and real-world applications of AI-driven SEO provides valuable insights into how these strategies translate into tangible results. By examining examples of companies that successfully integrated AI into their SEO efforts, we gain a clearer understanding of effective tactics, challenges overcome, and measurable outcomes. These case studies showcase how AI can be leveraged to enhance content optimization, predict user behavior, personalize user experiences, and improve overall search performance. In this chapter, we'll delve into real-world applications of AI in SEO, highlighting best practices, key learnings, and actionable takeaways that can inspire and inform your own AI-driven SEO strategy.

A. Success Stories of AI-Optimized SEO: Strategies Used and Results Achieved

Integrating artificial intelligence (AI) into search engine optimization (SEO) strategies has enabled various organizations to enhance their online presence and achieve significant results. Below are notable examples illustrating the strategies employed and the outcomes realized through AI-optimized SEO.

1. LinkedIn's Collaborative Articles

LinkedIn introduced AI-powered collaborative articles to foster engagement and share expert knowledge. These articles are initiated by AI, covering diverse topics, and are subsequently enriched by contributions from industry experts. This approach not only leverages AI for content generation but also incorporates human expertise to ensure quality and relevance. The initiative has successfully engaged over 1.5 million users, demonstrating the effectiveness of combining AI with human insights to enhance content quality and user engagement.

2. AI-Driven Content Creation for SEO

Several companies have adopted AI tools to streamline content creation processes, resulting in improved SEO performance. For instance, organizations have utilized AI to generate content that aligns with user intent and search engine algorithms, leading to higher rankings and increased organic traffic. These AI-driven strategies have enabled businesses to produce relevant content efficiently, catering to audience needs and enhancing visibility in search results.

3. AI-Powered Keyword Research and Optimization

AI tools have revolutionized keyword research by analyzing vast datasets to identify high-potential keywords and topics. Companies employing AI for keyword analysis have reported more effective targeting of user queries, resulting in improved search rankings and increased website traffic. By leveraging AI's analytical capabilities, businesses can optimize their content strategies to better meet user intent and stay ahead of competitors.

4. Enhancing User Experience with AI

AI has been instrumental in personalizing user experiences on websites, leading to higher engagement and conversion rates. By analyzing user behavior and preferences,

AI systems can tailor content and recommendations, making interactions more relevant and engaging. This personalization not only improves user satisfaction but also contributes to better SEO performance through increased dwell time and reduced bounce rates.

5. AI in Technical SEO Audits

AI-powered tools have streamlined technical SEO audits by quickly identifying issues such as broken links, crawl errors, and site speed problems. Companies utilizing AI for technical audits have been able to promptly address these issues, resulting in improved site performance and search engine rankings. The efficiency of AI in diagnosing and resolving technical SEO challenges allows businesses to maintain optimal website health and user experience.

These examples underscore the transformative impact of AI on SEO strategies, highlighting how AI-driven approaches can lead to substantial improvements in search performance, user engagement, and overall digital presence.

B. Lessons from Common Pitfalls: Mistakes to Avoid

Integrating artificial intelligence (AI) into search engine optimization (SEO) strategies offers significant advantages, but it's crucial to navigate potential pitfalls to ensure success. By examining common mistakes, businesses can proactively address challenges and optimize their AI-driven SEO efforts.

1. Overreliance on AI Without Human Oversight

While AI tools can automate and enhance various SEO tasks, depending solely on them without human supervision can lead to suboptimal outcomes. AI-generated content or recommendations may lack the nuance and contextual understanding that human expertise provides.

Lesson Learned: Maintain a balanced approach by combining AI capabilities with human judgment. Ensure that AI outputs are reviewed and refined by SEO professionals to align with brand voice and strategic objectives.

2. Neglecting Data Quality and Integration

AI systems rely heavily on data quality. Feeding AI tools with inaccurate, outdated, or incomplete data can result in misleading insights and ineffective strategies.

Lesson Learned: Invest in robust data management practices. Regularly audit and update data sources to ensure accuracy. Integrate AI tools with reliable data streams to enhance the quality of insights and recommendations.

3. Ignoring Ethical Considerations

Implementing AI without considering ethical implications can lead to issues such as biased content, privacy violations, or non-compliance with regulations.

Lesson Learned: Adopt ethical AI practices by ensuring transparency, fairness, and accountability in AI applications. Stay informed about relevant regulations and industry standards to maintain compliance and build trust with your audience.

4. Failing to Align AI Initiatives with Business Goals

Deploying AI tools without a clear strategy or alignment with business objectives can result in wasted resources and missed opportunities.

Lesson Learned: Define clear goals for AI integration that align with your overall SEO and business strategies. Establish key performance indicators (KPIs) to measure the effectiveness of AI-driven initiatives and adjust tactics as needed.

5. Underestimating the Need for Continuous Learning

AI and SEO are continually evolving. Failing to stay updated with the latest developments can render your strategies obsolete.

Lesson Learned: Commit to ongoing education and training for your team. Stay abreast of industry trends, AI advancements, and SEO best practices to adapt and refine your strategies effectively.

By recognizing and addressing these common pitfalls, businesses can harness the full potential of AI in their SEO strategies, leading to improved performance, user engagement, and competitive advantage.

C. Industry-Specific Insights: E-commerce, Services, B2B, and Local Businesses

Artificial intelligence (AI) is transforming search engine optimization (SEO) across various industries, offering tailored strategies to meet unique sector needs. Below is an exploration of AI-driven SEO applications in e-commerce, service-based businesses, B2B enterprises, and local businesses.

1. E-commerce

AI enhances SEO by optimizing product listings, personalizing user experiences, and predicting consumer behavior.

- **Product Optimization**: AI tools analyze customer reviews and search patterns to identify relevant keywords, improving product page rankings. For instance, AI-driven platforms can suggest keyword variations that align with current trends, enhancing visibility.

- **Personalized Recommendations**: AI algorithms assess user behavior to offer personalized product suggestions, increasing engagement and conversion rates. This personalization not only improves user satisfaction but also contributes to better SEO performance through increased dwell time and reduced bounce rates.

- **Inventory Management**: AI predicts demand trends, aiding in inventory optimization and ensuring product availability aligns with consumer interest, indirectly supporting SEO by maintaining customer satisfaction.

2. Service-Based Businesses

Service-oriented companies leverage AI to enhance local SEO, manage online reputations, and streamline customer interactions.

- **Local SEO Enhancement**: AI analyzes local search trends, enabling businesses to optimize content for regional keywords and improve visibility in local search results. This advancement allows businesses to target more specific, localized audiences and increase their visibility in local search results.

- **Reputation Management**: AI monitors online reviews and social media mentions, providing insights to address customer feedback promptly, which is crucial for maintaining a positive online presence.

- **Chatbots and Customer Service**: AI-powered chatbots handle inquiries efficiently, enhancing user experience and engagement, factors that positively influence SEO rankings.

3. Business-to-Business (B2B)

In the B2B sector, AI-driven SEO focuses on lead generation, content optimization, and understanding complex buyer journeys.

- **Lead Scoring**: AI evaluates potential leads based on behavior and engagement, allowing businesses to prioritize high-quality prospects and tailor SEO strategies accordingly.

- **Content Personalization**: AI analyzes visitor data to deliver personalized content, increasing relevance and engagement, leading to improved rankings.

- **Predictive Analytics**: AI forecasts market trends and buyer behavior, enabling proactive content creation and SEO adjustments to meet evolving demands.

4. Local Businesses

For local enterprises, AI enhances visibility in community searches and improves customer engagement.

- **Voice Search Optimization**: AI helps businesses adapt to the rise of voice search by identifying conversational keywords and common question phrases, improving chances of ranking for voice-activated searches.

- **Local Listings Management**: AI tools ensure business information is accurate across directories, crucial for local SEO success.

- **Customer Engagement**: AI analyzes local customer behavior, aiding in the creation of targeted marketing campaigns that resonate with the community.

By adopting AI-driven SEO strategies tailored to their specific industry needs, businesses can enhance their online presence, engage effectively with their target audience, and achieve sustainable growth.

Chapter 18. App Store Optimization (ASO) and SEO Integration

With the rapid growth of mobile applications, optimizing for app stores has become a crucial component of digital strategy. App Store Optimization (ASO) enhances an app's discoverability on app platforms like Apple's App Store and Google Play, while SEO ensures visibility on search engines. Combining ASO and SEO offers a powerful way to boost app visibility, attract more users, and support overall brand growth.

1. Unified Keyword Research for ASO and SEO

Conducting combined keyword research for ASO and SEO helps ensure that your app ranks well both in app stores and on search engines. A shared keyword strategy allows for broader visibility, capturing users who search for relevant terms on multiple platforms.

- **Identify Cross-Platform Keywords**: Start with an in-depth analysis to identify keywords popular on both app stores and search engines. Tools like Ahrefs, App Annie, and Sensor Tower provide data on keywords that perform well across different platforms.

- **Primary and Secondary Keyword Usage**: Include primary keywords in app titles, descriptions, and your website's meta tags and headers. Use secondary keywords in areas like update notes and product descriptions on the app store and in additional content on the landing page.

- **Localization for Global Reach**: Optimize keywords for different languages and regions to broaden your audience. Localized keywords help increase app visibility in international markets by meeting search and language preferences of specific user bases.

2. Optimizing App Descriptions and Landing Pages

A well-optimized app description in the app store, combined with a strong landing page on your website, creates a seamless experience for users and supports both ASO and SEO objectives.

- **App Store Descriptions**: Craft clear, keyword-optimized descriptions that highlight the app's core features and value. Regularly update descriptions to reflect new features, benefits, and major updates.

- **SEO-Optimized Landing Pages**: Create landing pages with detailed, engaging content about the app, optimized with high-value keywords. Use headings, bulleted lists, and clear call-to-actions (CTAs) that encourage users to download the app. Including user reviews, testimonials, and FAQs on the page can improve SEO and enhance user trust.

- **Link Building to Support ASO and SEO**: Generate quality backlinks to the landing page through collaborations with relevant blogs, influencers, and app reviewers. These backlinks increase traffic to the app's landing page, which can indirectly boost app store rankings by driving qualified traffic to download the app.

3. Enhancing Visual Assets for Better Engagement

High-quality visuals play a significant role in driving engagement on app stores and can also improve SEO performance on landing pages.

- **App Icon and Screenshots**: Create an eye-catching app icon that clearly represents your app's purpose. Use high-quality screenshots showcasing the app's key features and user interface. Visuals should meet the specific technical requirements of both the Apple App Store and Google Play.

- **App Preview Videos**: Develop a brief, engaging preview video to demonstrate the app's functionality and benefits. These videos can also be repurposed on social media and YouTube, driving additional traffic to the app and improving SEO.

- **Optimized Images for SEO**: Use alt text and captions on images embedded in your app's landing page to boost SEO performance. Properly optimized images can rank in image search results, increasing traffic to your landing page and improving user engagement.

4. Managing Reviews and Ratings for ASO and SEO Impact

Reviews and ratings are crucial to both ASO and SEO, as they build credibility and influence rankings on app stores.

- **Prompting User Reviews**: Use in-app prompts to encourage satisfied users to leave positive reviews, especially after key interactions, such as after completing a purchase or reaching a milestone in the app. Ensure prompts are unobtrusive to avoid disrupting the user experience.

- **Responding to Feedback**: Regularly monitor and respond to user feedback, especially negative reviews. Addressing user concerns not only improves ratings but also demonstrates your commitment to customer satisfaction.

- **Showcasing Reviews on Landing Pages**: Feature positive reviews and testimonials from the app store on your app's landing page. Use schema markup to display ratings in Google search results, which can improve click-through rates and add credibility to your landing page.

5. Tracking and Analyzing ASO and SEO Metrics

Monitoring both ASO and SEO metrics is essential for understanding the performance of your strategy and making data-driven adjustments.

- **ASO Metrics**: Use tools like App Annie, Mobile Action, or Sensor Tower to track app store rankings, keyword performance, and download metrics. Analyzing these metrics helps you identify which keywords and descriptions drive the most visibility and downloads.

- **SEO Analytics**: Use Google Analytics or similar tools to monitor traffic, conversions, and user behavior on your app's landing page. Pay attention to metrics like bounce rate, time on page, and conversion rates to understand which elements resonate with users.

- **Integrated Performance Insights**: Combining ASO and SEO data allows you to get a holistic view of your app's visibility and performance. Cross-referencing ASO data (like app downloads) with SEO data (like landing page traffic) provides insights into how users discover your app.

6. Key Resources and Tools for ASO and SEO Integration

Using the right tools and resources is essential to successfully integrate ASO and SEO strategies. Here are recommended tools for different stages of ASO and SEO:

- **Keyword Research**:
    - **Ahrefs**: Provides extensive keyword data for SEO, helping you identify terms to use on your landing page and app description.
    - **Sensor Tower and App Annie**: Dedicated ASO tools that offer keyword suggestions, competitor analysis, and search volume data specific to app stores.

- **App Store Optimization**:
    - **Mobile Action**: Helps track app store rankings, monitor competitors, and analyze keyword performance.
    - **SplitMetrics**: A/B testing tool for testing different visuals, descriptions, and layouts on app store listings to determine what drives the most engagement and downloads.

- **Analytics and Performance Tracking**:
    - **Google Analytics**: Essential for tracking traffic, behavior, and conversions on your app's landing page.
    - **AppTweak**: Provides detailed ASO analytics, including keyword rankings and user ratings trends, to help improve app store performance.
    - **AppFollow**: Tracks app store reviews, ratings, and keywords in real time, enabling you to monitor customer feedback and respond.

- **Review Management**:
    - **AppFollow and Appbot**: These tools help aggregate reviews from different app stores, making it easier to monitor feedback and respond to user concerns promptly.

Bringing It All Together: Crafting a Unified ASO and SEO Strategy

Integrating ASO with SEO creates a unified strategy that maximizes app visibility and engagement across both app stores and search engines. By aligning keyword research, optimizing visual assets, managing reviews, and tracking metrics with specialized tools, businesses can improve discoverability, enhance user trust, and ultimately drive more downloads. This cohesive approach to ASO and SEO ensures that users can find and engage with your app seamlessly, helping you stand out in an increasingly competitive digital marketplace.

Chapter 19. Conclusion

The integration of artificial intelligence in SEO demands a more sophisticated approach to optimizing for both traditional search engines and AI-driven platforms. This guide has provided a comprehensive exploration of SEO strategies in the age of AI, from foundational on-page and off-page factors to advanced techniques tailored for AI search engines, voice search, and app store optimization. By understanding and applying these strategies, businesses can stay ahead of the curve, enhance their online visibility, and engage more effectively with their target audiences. As you implement these insights, remember that SEO is an ongoing process—one that requires continuous learning, adaptation, and fine-tuning to meet the ever-changing expectations of both users and search algorithms.

A. The Ongoing Evolution of SEO and AI

Embracing Change and Innovation

The intersection of SEO and AI marks an exciting and transformative period for digital marketing. As AI technologies continue to advance, search engines are becoming increasingly sophisticated, able to interpret context, predict user intent, and personalize results on an unprecedented scale. This evolution demands that SEO strategies remain adaptable and innovative, moving beyond traditional tactics to encompass user-centric, data-driven approaches.

Embracing this change means staying informed about the latest developments in machine learning, natural language processing, and AI-powered search platforms. It also involves a willingness to experiment with emerging tools, continually test new strategies, and refine practices based on user behavior and algorithm shifts. SEO professionals who remain proactive in learning and adapting are better positioned to leverage AI's full potential, ensuring their digital presence remains resilient and impactful.

B. Empowering Businesses in the Digital Age

Taking Control of Your Online Presence

In today's digital era, a strong online presence is no longer optional—it's essential for business success. AI-driven SEO empowers businesses to actively shape their visibility, reach, and brand reputation across search engines and AI platforms. By harnessing AI tools and data insights, businesses can better understand their audiences, anticipate needs, and engage users with personalized, relevant content.

Taking control of your online presence involves a strategic approach to SEO that encompasses technical optimization, high-quality content, and a deep understanding of user intent. Businesses that prioritize a comprehensive SEO strategy not only improve search rankings but also build credibility and trust with their audiences. Through ongoing optimization and a proactive mindset, companies can leverage AI to become more agile, adapt to changes in user behavior and technology, and stay ahead of the competition in the digital age.

C. Final Thoughts and Encouragement

The Importance of Persistence and Adaptation

SEO in the age of AI demands persistence and adaptability. Success comes from consistent effort, strategic planning, and openness to change as technology and user behaviors evolve. As AI reshapes search and online interaction, staying agile is key for businesses aiming to maintain a strong digital presence. Though challenging, optimizing for AI-powered search offers valuable opportunities to connect with audiences. By embracing change, testing strategies, and refining your approach, SEO can become a powerful growth tool, building visibility, credibility, and success in a dynamic digital world.

www.ingramcontent.com/pod-product-compliance
Lightning Source LLC
Chambersburg PA
CBHW052308220526
45472CB00001B/26